THE Lazy GOURMET

Real Food. Real Easy.

MARJORIE GELB

WITH

JOSIE A.G. SHAPIRO

ILLUSTRATIONS BY STEPHANIE GELB

THE LAZY GOURMET: REAL FOOD. REAL EASY.

FIRST EDITION

DESIGNED BY SARAH CISTON

PUBLISHED BY WATCHWORD PRESS

Printed on acid-free paper.

Library of Congress Cataloging-in-Publication Data
available upon request.

ISBN 978-0-9842280-1-0

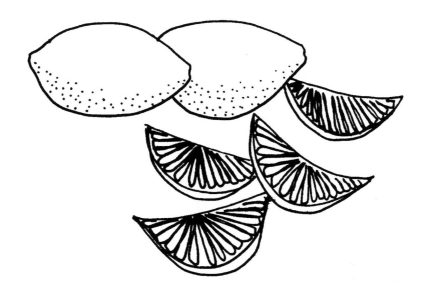

Table of Contents

To my husband, Mark,
who appreciates every bite,
who tackles every dirty dish,
and who has my whole heart.

Introduction to
THE Lazy GOURMET

I'm a Lazy Gourmet. I love great food, and back in the day I attended classes at the Cordon Bleu in France. Studying the French classics led me to labor-intensive preparations of things like Duck à l'Orange, *croquembouche*, and Veal Oscar. Years later, as a full-time working lawyer raising two kids, I still retained my love of good food. However, I no longer had the time and the energy to prepare it. I couldn't come home from a stressful job and make complicated meals. And we certainly couldn't afford to eat out every night. What's a gourmet to do? My solution: I developed a cooking style that I call pure lazy.

The French definition of a *gourmet* is someone who likes to eat good things. Julia Child, in her tome *Mastering the Art of French Cooking*, wrote that her book was for the American cook who is looking for "something wonderful to eat." I'm that person—when I cook, I want the food to be not only good, but wonderful. The part of me that is gourmet uses only first-quality ingredients: fresh produce, vibrant herbs and spices, and the best and freshest fish, chicken, and meat. I mostly avoid canned and frozen products because they usually taste stale and bland. I use classic techniques because they preserve the natural qualities of the ingredients I use.

Yet I am lazy.

While lazy is in the eye of the beholder, I think we can all agree that there are several things that make cooking work-intensive, that is, not lazy:

1. Shopping
2. Lots of chopping
3. Lots of steps
4. Washing dishes

Finding recipes that minimized these chores but produced wonderful dishes became my hobby. You might even call it an obsession. Over my 40 years or so of serious cooking, I have amassed a considerable number of recipes that meet these criteria. Some of them are straight from the source; even Julia Child has a few recipes that are simple (see Leg of Lamb with Mustard Crust, page 146). Some of them I have adapted—i.e. cut every corner I could from a traditional recipe (see Boeuf Bourguignon, page 134). Some I have collected from fellow travelers, i.e. moms in a hurry (thanks, Alice, for your Gazpacho, page 38, and Pots de Crème, page 155). And finally, some recipes I invented. This book is a collection of the best gourmet recipes that can safely be called "lazy."

Does the world need another cookbook? I think so. While I am now a semi-retired grandmother, I see my daughters and their friends going through what I did. They are beginning to climb their career ladders and establish their households. Why should they have to reinvent the wheel when feeding their families? Why should I take this culinary goldmine to the grave? My daughter Josie, a new mom, has been testing these recipes formally and informally for years. She helped me set my thoughts on paper for this book — a perfect project for her because, while cooking and entering cooking contests is her hobby, she is the laziest of gourmets. She even buys her ginger pre-grated and in a bottle. Many of the shortcuts in these recipes are hers. My daughter Molly does not cook but is fortunate in her romantic choice (her husband does the cooking). He has perfected Red Lentil Soup (page 41), makes it

three times a week, and aspires to expand his repertoire. My friend Katie, also a new mom and a brilliant lawyer, cannot figure out how to follow a complicated recipe. I promised to help. This book is for these people, and for all the other lazy gourmets out there.

Who is a lazy gourmet and who will benefit from this book?

A lazy gourmet likes good food and knows it when she tastes it.

A lazy gourmet wants to know what is in the food she eats and wants to serve healthy food. Fast food and packaged food may taste okay, but can be loaded with salt and sugar and mysterious chemicals. My husband has a family history of heart problems. From the get-go I eliminated as much cream and butter as possible from even my beloved French recipes.

A lazy gourmet likes to cook. This is not the *I Hate to Cook Book*. With all due respect to its author Peg Bracken, whose Stroganoff comes highly recommended by my foodie/slacker sister, using canned cream of chicken soup does not make the grade.

A lazy gourmet knows how to cook. She does not need to be told that chicken needs to be cooked until done.

A lazy gourmet does not need to prepare a meal in 30 minutes every night. She is concerned about the quality of the time, not necessarily the quantity. Easy Vegetarian Chili (page 92) cooks for four hours, but requires very little work, feeds the family for a week, and tastes fabulous.

A lazy gourmet is not a purist. She is willing to cut out steps, cut corners, and use labor-saving equipment.

A lazy gourmet is not a spendthrift but knows that time is money and that you can buy pre-peeled garlic, pre-peeled shrimp and pre-chopped onions. The butcher will cut up a first quality organic chicken at no extra cost. Peeled shrimp and garlic without the skin usually cost more, but if it will save you some time, why not? When it makes economic sense and suits your budget, I say go for it.

What will you NOT find in a Lazy Gourmet recipe?

A lazy recipe will not call for any obscure ingredient. Going from store to store looking for *nuoc man* (Vietnamese fish sauce) if you do not live in a culturally diverse area is not lazy. Further, shopping can be reduced by using ingredients with a long shelf life like pasta, rice, onions, garlic, spices, anchovies, olives, and dried fruit, or a relatively long refrigerator life, like tomato paste in a tube, lemons, carrots, celery, hard cheese, or Asian bottled ingredients.

A lazy recipe will not have lots of steps.

A lazy recipe will not call for lots of dishes, pots, pans, or utensils. Full disclosure: in my household, my husband does all the dishes. All the dishes, all the time. I have nonetheless tried to be sensitive to those not similarly blessed.

Essential Lazy Equipment

Buy the best equipment you can afford. It makes the task at hand easier, which is the Lazy Gourmet's goal.

- **Knives:** You need a really good chef's knife (around 8 inches) and a paring knife. No matter what brand you choose, the important thing is to keep your knives sharp with a steel or by bringing them to a sharpening service every so often. Dull blades prolong chopping time and can make even an extremely lazy recipe quite frustrating.
- **Horizontal vegetable peelers:** You need to abandon that old-fashioned vertical peeler and

get a horizontal one (also called a Y-shaped or U-shaped peeler). As my daughter would say, "they rock," and they make peeling squash and potatoes almost lazy.

• **Non-stick sauté pan:** A good sauté pan helps food brown quickly. Non-stick pans can be cheap. Julia Child herself was a devotee: I saw an interview with her in which she confessed that her relatively cheap non-stick frying pan was her favorite. Food cooked in a non-stick pan forms a crust that won't tear and it will save time at cleanup.

• **Mini food processor:** It's really hard to eliminate all chopping, but a mini-food processor will help. This is an essential lazy tool. It doesn't take up much room on the counter, and if the recipe calls for more than one clove of garlic I find it saves a lot of time. It is also great for mincing ginger or shallots, or for blending garlic and herbs together, or for making a creamy vinaigrette. Of course, it also creates another dish to wash (although most are dishwasher safe), so whether you choose to use one depends completely on what feels lazier to you—fewer dishes to clean or less time spent chopping.

• **Large food processor:** Another essential for chopping and making cakes, mousses, pie crusts, some cookies, sauces, and dips. It is also good for slicing and shredding. Older food processors do not work well for soups because they leak, but newer versions do the job just fine.

• **Immersion blender:** This tool serves the same function as a food processor but is particularly handy for soups, and is a lot easier to clean than the blender.

• **Pressure cooker:** This is not essential, but cuts cooking time by two thirds. It's great for making quick vegetable soups and 7-minute risotto. I'm a fan, though there is the cleanup factor, and pressure cookers are a major investment.

• **Large zip lock bags:** Perfect for marinating meat, chicken, and fish with no messy cleanup afterwards. (If you have an environmental conscience, you can rinse them out for reuse and store them in the freezer. If you don't, toss them and hope someone will make biodegradable ones soon.)

- **Garlic press:** I use a lot of garlic. With the press, you can mash it instead of chopping and you don't have to remove the peel. Purists may balk.

- **Microplane® grater:** A relatively new invention. Great for grating lemon peel and hard cheeses like Parmesan.

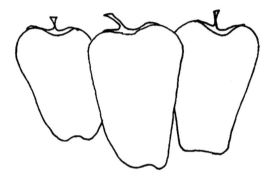

Essential Cooking Ingredients for the Lazy Gourmet

As with equipment, always use the highest quality ingredients you can afford. Good ingredients make a recipe taste good with very little extra effort. Thus the trick to being a lazy gourmet is to shop infrequently but well.

- **Fresh produce:** Nowadays most people can go to farmers' markets in the spring and summer (and in California we're lucky enough to be able to go year-round). But even at the big supermarkets, fresh vegetables are brought in regularly, so there's really no excuse not to use them. And most fresh produce will sit happily in the refrigerator for a week, so you don't need to go shopping every day.

What follows is a list of ingredients that you can easily keep on hand without shopping for them on a weekly basis.

- **Fresh herbs:** Fresh parsley, basil, sage, thyme, and rosemary can make a real difference in a recipe. You can buy packages of fresh herbs in most grocery stores. But if you grow them yourself in the garden or in pots in the house, they'll always be available and you won't have to go shopping for a spur-of-the-moment recipe.

• **Lemons:** You may be surprised at how often a lemon comes to the rescue of a recipe or sauce that needs a little zing. The trick is to keep lemons on hand at all times, and restock them regularly. If you live in California, you or one of your neighbors probably has a Meyer lemon tree (and if you don't, you should think about getting one). Think about the shopping you won't have to do.

• **Cheese:** Parmesan, cheddar, mozzarella, and Monterey Jack all keep for a long time in the refrigerator, carefully wrapped and (rewrapped after use). You can even grate your own cheese in advance and store it in jars or storage containers. This won't keep as long as store-bought grated cheese, but at least you know you are using good cheese with good flavor and texture, and not the tasteless kind usually sold in bags and jars.

• **Onions, shallots, and garlic:** Keep them in the house as staples. They don't have to be refrigerated and they last quite a long time when stored in a dark, cool place.

• **Tomato paste in a tube:** This ingredient is incredibly useful when you just need a little push of tomatoes. It used to be available only in Italian grocery stores but now you can get it anywhere.

• **Canned tomatoes:** The sad truth is that tomatoes are only fabulous for a few months every year. During those months my family eats them so often that we almost get sick of them. But during the other months I find that high-end canned whole tomatoes, and even diced tomatoes, are excellent, especially when they are cooked for a long time (see Penne Casserole with Two Cheeses, page 86).

• **Anchovies:** There is a big difference between a mediocre tinned anchovy and a nice plump one. I personally prefer the ones that come in olive oil in glass jars because I don't like to rinse and soak the salted ones, but not everyone is as lazy as I.

• **Canned or packaged chicken, beef, and vegetarian stock:** This is where I leave the more persnickety cooks behind. Making your own stock is not hard, and is actually very satisfying, but it is not really lazy. You have to buy ingredients that you may not have in the house; you have to simmer for the right amount of time; you have to strain and cool and degrease (for chicken stock anyway), and pour the finished stock into containers and freeze. So I buy stock. I buy good brands with low sodium and fat. I keep lots in the house. Over time I have come to prefer some brands—and you will too. Keep track of the ones you like and the ones you don't. Stock in cubes can be very convenient, but is also very salty. If you do use stock in cubes, use less than the recipes suggest and omit any other salt until you've tasted the finished dish.

• **Frozen spinach and peas:** The Lazy Gourmet doesn't really buy fresh peas. They're only really sweet for a few hours and are tedious to shell (and frozen peas are often quite good.) I cook fresh spinach (which you can buy prewashed in a bag) quite often, but one-pound bags of frozen chopped spinach come in handy in lots of recipes and are easy to keep in the freezer.

• **Frozen meat and poultry:** Before freezing, seal fresh meat (still in the butcher's wrapping) in a zip lock bag. If using prepackaged chicken or meat, remove it from the packaging, divide into serving portions, wrap in plastic wrap (to prevent freezer burn), and freeze in zip lock bags. Frozen meat is best used within 3 months of freezing. The downside (as compared with fresh meat) is that you have to remember to defrost it—but then again, you won't have to go to the grocery store.

• **Canned white, red, and black beans and garbanzos:** It's not hard to cook beans. It usually requires soaking overnight (but not in the Easy Vegetarian Chili recipe, page 92), and cooking for an hour or two. Cooked beans can be frozen. Nevertheless, I keep canned beans in the house. You can never tell when you'll need to add beans to a salad for protein or make hummus in a hurry.

• **Rice, lentils, couscous, quinoa, pasta, and dried beans:** There are actually many varieties of all of these grains and they have very long shelf lives. If you keep them in the house, you will cut down on emergency shopping and increase your ability to throw something together at the last minute.

• **Other flavor boosters:** Olives, capers, Lan Chi Chili Paste with Garlic, soy sauce, red pepper flakes, tahini, and nuts all last a long time in the fridge or on the shelf (or in the case of nuts, in the freezer), and add a lot of flavor and pizzazz to many recipes.

A Few Words About Everyday Ingredients

Over time, most cooks develop preferences about their everyday ingredients. I have mine. I'll list them, just so you know.

• **Salt:** I use kosher salt because I read that it dissolves faster than sea salt. It is a little saltier in taste, so you may use less than you do of sea salt.

• **Butter:** Unsalted butter, which I prefer, lets you control the amount of salt in your food. Also, it seems to me to be fresher in taste. Throughout the recipes, however, I have simply called for "butter," so you can make your own choice. The exception comes in the dessert chapter, where unsalted butter is a necessity.

• **Eggs:** I use large eggs. They're not better, but for consistency you should use the same size eggs every time.

• **Red peppers:** I prefer the taste of home roasted and peeled red peppers. I buy four at a time when they're on sale, put them under a broiler, turn them when they get brown, and then put them in a glass bowl covered with plastic wrap to steam and cool. Then I just slip the skins off, remove the seeds, and store them in the fridge or the freezer. I have some store-bought peeled red peppers in the larder for emergencies. I don't like peppers stored in vinegar because I don't think the vinegar completely rinses off and the flavor is aggressive.

• **Parsley and cilantro:** Many Lazy Gourmet recipes call for parsley or cilantro leaves. I do not usually pick off the leaves one by one. After rinsing the herbs, I roughly cut off the leaves and tender stems from the top and sides. If they're minced, I don't think anyone notices.

• **Herbs and spices:** I like to taste the herbs and spices that I use, so I often cook with more than is called for in the recipe. I keep adding and tasting until the flavor really comes through.

Timing

An ordinary gourmet will spend any amount of time making a nice meal. The Lazy Gourmet wants to limit the actual amount of work, but is less concerned with a recipe's marinating, cooking, or resting time. While the food rests, you rest. I have indicated in my recipes how much time involves actual work. I call this "prep time." In addition, the food may cook, unattended ("cooking time") or cool unattended ("cooling time") or even rest unattended in the refrigerator or on the counter ("resting time").

Happy Cooking!

Many of the recipes in this book have already been shared with my discerning but busy friends. People tell me that the recipes are wonderful and have entered into their family's regular repertoire. I have always considered a cookbook a success if I find one or two recipes I use regularly. I hope you find dozens.

Appetizers

MUSTARD GRUYÈRE CRACKERS
PARMESAN CRISPS
HUMMUS
BABA GHANOUSH
BLUE CHEESE BALL
SMOKED TROUT PÂTÉ
ALMOND RED PEPPER DIP
UNCLE HARRY'S CHOPPED CHICKEN LIVER
PROSCIUTTO AND GRUYÈRE PINWHEELS

The only problem with throwing a dinner party with appetizers is that if you stuff people with pre-table snacks, they won't be hungry come mealtime. Then again, schmoozing and lounging on couches is a wonderful way to launch an event, and I'm certainly not going to preach appetizer abstinence.

The trick with hors d'oeuvres is to think them through. They shouldn't be a last-minute addition to your menu, but an integral part of it. If you're serving a heavier meal like Chicken with Olives, Prunes, and Capers (page 127), then don't overload your guests with equally weighty appetizers like the wonderful-but-better-for-a-potluck Blue Cheese Ball (page 22). Instead, try something lighter like Parmesan Crisps (page 19), or Hummus (page 20), or Baba Ghanoush (page 21) with carrots. Of course, if dinner is light, like grilled fish, then by all means, go wild with the cheese ball.

While all the recipes in this section can be made or prepped in advance, sometimes I laze out so completely I just serve simple store bought items like Japanese rice crackers, baby carrots, olives, dolmas, or shrimp with cocktail sauce. If you are feeling lazy-adventurous, however, read on, pre-cook, and enjoy.

MUSTARD GRUYÈRE CRACKERS

These crackers tend to make an impression far beyond their actual difficulty. You make the mixture in the food processor, roll it in plastic wrap, and wait until you need to slice and bake. The slice and bake time is 15 minutes. The mustard-Gruyère mixture has a long expiration date and can be made up to 3 days in advance, or frozen for a month.

1/2 pound Gruyere cheese
1/2 cup (1 stick) unsalted butter, softened and cut into 3 or 4 pieces
3 tablespoons grainy mustard
1 cup all-purpose flour

1. In a food processor, shred the cheese. Take out the shredding blade, dump the shredded cheese onto a plate and put in the knife blade. Return the cheese to the processor bowl.
2. Add the butter and mustard to the cheese and process a few seconds. The mixture will be lumpy.
3. Add flour and process until a soft dough forms.
4. Using a spatula, scoop the dough out of the processor bowl onto a clean surface or a plate. Divide the dough in half and place each half on a piece of plastic wrap. Use the wrap to form each piece of dough into a log 1½ inches in diameter log and around 4 or 5 inches long. You can push the dough together without touching it with your hands. Wrap the logs completely in plastic wrap and refrigerate until firm, at least one hour and up to 3 days.
5. When ready to cook, preheat oven to 350 degrees. With a sharp chef's knife, slice the log into ¼ inch-thick "crackers." Place on cookie sheet (no greasing or parchment paper necessary) and bake 15 minutes. Cool on a rack.

Prep time: 15 minutes
Waiting time: At least an hour
Cooking time: 15 minutes
Makes 36 crackers

PARMESAN CRISPS

With a very simple recipe like this one, the quality of the crisps is entirely dependent on the quality of the ingredients. Parmigiano-Reggiano is the best imported Parmesan cheese you can buy.

1/2 pound Parmigiano-Reggiano, shredded using the small holes on a hand grater or a handheld round Mouli grater
Whole black peppercorns, in grinder

1. Preheat oven to 350 degrees. Line two cookie sheets with parchment paper.
2. Spoon cheese in 2-tablespoon mounds on cookie sheet, placing each mound of cheese 3 inches apart from its neighbor. With the back of a spoon, carefully flatten cheese mounds into circles 3 inches in diameter. Grind one or two turns of the peppermill on top of each cheese circle.
3. Bake 10-12 minutes, until crisps are light brown all over. Let cool on the pan to harden, about 5 minutes.

Prep time: 5 minutes
Cooking time: 12 minutes
Cooling time: 5 minutes
Makes 18 crisps

HUMMUS

Never underestimate the dazzle factor. While you can certainly buy good quality hummus, guests are often thrilled that you went to the trouble to make it yourself. If you stock up on the canned garbanzo beans and tahini, and the other staples in this recipe, you can make this tasty dip and sandwich spread on the fly, anytime. Once you're comfortable with the basic recipe, get wild and introduce your own spices to taste: roasted red bell peppers for a sweeter, pale red hummus; Kalamata olives for a Greek spin.

3 cloves garlic, peeled
2 cups cooked garbanzo beans (chickpeas) (one 15-oz. can)
2/3 cup tahini (toasted sesame butter), stirred if it has separated
2 1/2 tablespoons ground cumin
1/2 cup water
1/2 cup fresh lemon juice (more if necessary)
2 tablespoons extra virgin olive oil
1/2 teaspoon salt
10 turns freshly ground black pepper
1/4 cup chopped parsley or cilantro (optional)

1. In a food processor, mince the garlic.
2. Rinse the garbanzo beans in a colander under cold water. Add them to the garlic and process. Add the tahini, cumin, ½ cup water, the lemon juice, olive oil, and salt and pepper. Process at least one minute, until the hummus is very smooth. Taste the mixture and adjust the seasonings. Stir in cilantro or parsley just before serving. Serve with baby carrots, pita bread, or crackers.

Total time: 20 minutes
Makes 2 cups
Serves 12 or more

BABA GHANOUSH

Eggplant is often saturated with oil, because oil is an easy way to make this underappreciated vegetable tender. Enter the microwave. Forget the fat and rely on pure molecular heat to soften your eggplant. Mash the whole thing up with some refreshing lemon juice, garlic, and just a dollop of tahini, and you'll have a nice healthy dip that even the most diligent dieters can appreciate.

1 large eggplant, around 1 pound
3 cloves garlic
2 tablespoons parsley leaves and small stems, loosely packed
2 tablespoons lemon juice
1/2 teaspoon ground cumin
1 teaspoon salt
10 turns freshly ground black pepper
2-3 tablespoons tahini, stirred if it has separated

1. Prick the eggplant all over with a fork. (Don't skip this step or the eggplant might explode.) On a plate or a piece of waxed paper, cook in microwave on high for 9-12 minutes, until it has collapsed. Cut the eggplant in half lengthwise and let cool to room temperature. (Or bake the eggplant in an oven for 45 minutes at 450 degrees.)
2. Mince together garlic and parsley. Spoon the flesh out of the skin of the eggplant, and mash in a bowl with a fork. Add the lemon juice, cumin, salt, pepper, and tahini along with the minced garlic and parsley. Taste and adjust seasoning.
3. Cool to room temperature. Serve on pita bread or with crackers.

Prep time: 15 minutes
Cooking time: 10 minutes (in the microwave)
Cooling time: 30 minutes
Makes 2 cups
Serves 8 or more

BLUE CHEESE BALL

Talk about your perfect potluck food—there's no bigger hit at a party than a big ball of cheese. And this particular cheese ball happens to look quite attractive, with chopped nuts adorning its exterior edge. How's that for dressing up?

2 cloves garlic, peeled
2 small slices onion
1/4 of a red bell pepper
8 ounces sharp cheddar
8 ounces low-fat cream cheese
4 ounces Roquefort (French blue cheese)
1 tablespoon lemon juice
15 turns freshly ground black pepper
1/2 cup finely chopped pecans

1. In a food processor, chop garlic, onion, and pepper. Set aside.
2. In the same food processor, shred cheddar cheese. Remove the shredder blade and dump the shredded cheese onto a plate.
3. Switch in the regular blade again and process the cream cheese, blue cheese, lemon juice, and black pepper. Add the reserved grated cheddar cheese and combine well. Add the garlic, onion, and pepper. Process until combined.
4. Line a small round bowl with plastic wrap, leaving excess wrap draped over bowl edge. Put cheese mixture in bowl and cover completely with excess wrap. After the cheese has firmed up, use the wrap to form cheese into a round ball. Refrigerate for at least 2 hours to blend the flavors. The ball will keep covered in the refrigerator 3 days or so.
5. Before serving, pat the ball into a round shape, remove plastic wrap, and roll ball gently in chopped pecans.

Prep time: 20 minutes
Resting time: at least 2 hours
Serves 20

SMOKED TROUT PÂTÉ

Smoked trout is not quite imperishable, but will keep for weeks at a time. As will almost everything else in this recipe (save the parsley, which tends to wilt)—so you can just blend and serve. Pâté couldn't be easier.

1/2 small onion, or 3 shallots
1 cup parsley leaves
6 ounces smoked trout, skinned and with any bones picked out
6 ounces cream cheese (low-fat is okay; non-fat is not okay)
1/4 cup low-fat mayonnaise
2 tablespoons fresh lemon juice
15 turns freshly ground black pepper
Salt, to taste
Chives for garnish (optional)

1. In food processor, mince onion and parsley.
2. Add smoked trout, cream cheese, mayonnaise, lemon juice, and pepper to processor. Pulse until the mixture is well combined. Taste and adjust seasoning (the trout will be salty so you may not need extra salt). Place pâté in a serving bowl. Garnish with chives.

Serve with bread or crackers.

Total time: 15 minutes
Makes 2 cups
Serves 20

ALMOND RED PEPPER DIP

I usually prefer homemade skinned red peppers for their charred taste. But the ones in a jar are ten times lazier and work beautifully in this recipe.

3 cloves garlic
2 cups whole almonds, lightly toasted (or purchase roasted almonds)
1 teaspoon cumin
1/2 teaspoon sugar
1 teaspoon salt
1 12-ounce jar roasted red peppers, rinsed and drained, or
　　3 roasted and peeled red peppers, seeds and membranes
　　discarded
3 tablespoons extra virgin olive oil
3 tablespoons fresh lemon juice

1. In food processor, mince the garlic. Add the almonds and pulse until chopped. Add the cumin, sugar, and salt and continue to process until the nuts are ground finely.
2. Add the red peppers, the olive oil, and lemon juice. Pulse until smooth.
3. Taste and adjust the seasoning, adding more salt, oil, or lemon juice if needed.
4. Chill before serving.

Serve with crackers, toast, or raw vegetables.

Prep time: 15 minutes
Chilling time: at least 2 hours
Makes 2 cups
Serves 20

UNCLE HARRY'S CHOPPED CHICKEN LIVER

This is really my sister's recipe, although our Uncle Harry was the original creator. His version used schmaltz (rendered chicken fat), but you look me in the eye and tell me that seven tablespoons of butter isn't an improvement. When this recipe was included in my niece's school cookbook, the ingredient list called for "cologne" instead of "cognac." I like to think of the dads at that school tasting Uncle Harry's chopped liver and saying, "Hmm, smells familiar..."

3 eggs, hard-boiled and peeled
7 tablespoons unsalted butter, divided
1 medium onion, chopped
1 pound chicken livers, picked over to remove fat and liver spots
2 tablespoons Cognac
1 teaspoon salt
15 turns freshly ground black pepper

1. Melt 3 tablespoons of the butter in saucepan. Leave the rest of the butter out to soften. Sauté the onion until softened but not brown. Add the chicken livers and cook over medium-high heat until the livers are no longer red inside and have stiffened slightly, 3-5 minutes. Let the mixture cool a few minutes.
2. Place the chicken liver mixture, the hard-boiled eggs, the remaining 4 tablespoons of butter, cognac, salt, and pepper in the bowl of a food processor. Process on and off until smooth (but not too smooth— the mixture should have some texture).
3. Spoon into a mold or a bowl, cover tightly with plastic wrap, and refrigerate until firm, at least two hours and up to several days.
4. Unmold and serve with crackers or toast squares.

Prep time: 30 minutes (not counting hard-boiling the eggs, which you should do the night before anyway). Cooling time: 2 hours. Makes around 3 cups. Serves 12.

PROSCIUTTO AND GRUYÈRE PINWHEELS

Puff pastry may sound intimidating, but remember, you're defrosting it here, not making it from scratch. These pinwheels take a short time to prep and are ideal for a dinner party because you can make them as many as three days in advance before slicing and baking. Timing when prepping for a party is key, and this tasty but elegant appetizer makes your first course a breeze.

1 puff pastry sheet from a 17 1/2-ounce box, defrosted
1 egg, lightly beaten
2-3 ounces thinly sliced prosciutto
3/4 cup finely grated Gruyere cheese
1 1/3 tablespoons finely chopped fresh sage leaves

1. Cut pastry sheet in half horizontally to make two rectangular pieces. Place one half on a cutting board or lightly floured table so that the long side is facing you. Using a pastry brush dipped in egg, paint a strip along the far edge of the pastry sheet.
2. Cover the pastry (except for the egg strip) with slices of prosciutto. Mix the grated cheese with the chopped sage leaves. Sprinkle half the cheese mixture over the prosciutto. Starting at the edge closest to you, roll the pastry sheet tightly around the filling and pinch the eggy edge to seal. Repeat with the second half of the pastry.
3. Wrap each roll separately in plastic wrap and refrigerate at least 2 hours and up to 3 days.
4. Preheat oven to 400 degrees. Line two cookie sheets with parchment. Cut the rolls into ½-inch slices and place 2 inches apart on cookie sheets, pinwheel design facing up. Bake 14-16 minutes, or until nicely browned. Serve warm.

Prep time: 15 minutes
Cooking time: 15 minutes
Chilling time: 2 hours
Makes 38 pieces

Salads

BASIC SALAD DRESSING
ELEGANT SALAD WITH FRUIT, NUTS, AND CHEESE
WHITE BEAN AND SPINACH SALAD
CANNELLINI BEAN, AVOCADO, AND TOMATO SALAD
BEAN AND CORN SALAD
WILD RICE AND SMOKED CHICKEN SALAD
FARRO, TOMATO, AND MOZZARELLA SALAD
CHICKEN SALAD WITH OLIVE VINAIGRETTE

In the olden days, before supermarket packaging got out of control, the most time-consuming part of making salads was washing lettuce. Peel the leaves from the head, drench them under the faucet, cram them into a salad spinner, and twirl. Suddenly a one-bowl meal became a three-part trial. Now thanks to prewashed, prechopped, or plastic-wrapped lettuce (a.k.a. "Yuppie Chow"), salad is a cinch. For the average lazy cook, store-bought salad dressing makes these one-dish wonders extra simple, but for the Lazy Gourmet, making your own is key.

BASIC SALAD DRESSING

You can use any type of vinegar in your dressings, but when it comes to lazy elegance I recommend sherry vinegar with its slightly sweet, full-nosed flavor. If sherry vinegar isn't a staple in your cupboard, a combination of red wine vinegar and balsamic vinegar makes a nice substitute. Don't be afraid to play around with this basic recipe. Substitute shallot instead of the garlic for a more kissable flavor, and double or triple the recipe if you plan to eat salads the rest of the week. The final product will keep in the refrigerator for a week or more. My daughter has been known to use a single batch for weeks—she has no fear.

1-2 cloves garlic, peeled
3 tablespoons vinegar (red wine, balsamic, sherry, or a combination)
2 teaspoons Dijon mustard
Salt and pepper, to taste
1/2 cup extra virgin olive oil
1 tablespoon fresh herbs, leaves only

1. Drop the garlic clove into a small food processor or blender and mince. (Or, mince the garlic by hand and place in a small bowl.)
2. Add the vinegar, Dijon mustard, salt and pepper to the processor bowl. Let liquids sit a minute to dissolve the salt. Process or whisk a few seconds.
3. Add the oil in a thin stream while the food processor is running or beat small amounts of oil into the vinegar with a whisk until emulsified.
4. Add the herbs and process, or mince herbs and add to the dressing.

Note: For extra lazy salad dressing, place 3 tablespoons of the vinegar in a small jar, add salt and freshly ground black pepper to taste, 2 teaspoons of Dijon mustard, and shake the jar. Add ½ cup extra virgin olive oil and shake again. That's it. The dressing will emulsify.

Total time: 5 minutes
Makes 3/4 cup

ELEGANT SALAD WITH FRUIT, NUTS, AND CHEESE

Fruit and cheese salads just scream sophistication, so this one often appears on my fancy dinner table (or a potluck table or picnic basket). One day my friends will get sick of it, but not yet…. probably because no one worth their weight in cheese has ever said no to a nice Roquefort.

3-4 cups prewashed bagged greens
1/2 cup lightly toasted pecans or hazelnuts, whole or halved
1 cup diced fruit (apples or pears), or 1 cup dried cherries or cranberries
1/2 cup blue cheese (I prefer Roquefort), cut into small pieces
3 tablespoons Basic Salad Dressing, made with good-quality sherry vinegar

1. Put salad greens in bowl.
2. Add nuts, fruit, and cheese.
3. Just before serving, add salad dressing and toss.

Total time: 5-10 minutes, depending on whether you're dicing the fruit or not
Serves 3-6

WHITE BEAN AND SPINACH SALAD

My younger daughter is a vegetarian and so are all her friends. I suppose that's what comes from raising kids in Berkeley, but it's not something I bargained for when I decided to reproduce. Thanks to this salad, however, I can serve meat as a main course and still feel I've done my job as an all-inclusive, accommodating mother. With beans for protein, roasted red pepper for heft, Kalamata olives for salty flavor, and spinach as a vitamin-strong alternative to lettuce, this salad could be a pain in the butt to put together if not for some tried, true, and lazy shortcuts. The beans must be canned and the roasted red peppers can be pre-roasted or come from jars (the kind packed in water, not vinegar). Then all you have to do is buy pitted Kalamata olives. To be lazy you must use spinach that is washed, dried, and sealed in a bag.

1 tablespoon extra virgin olive oil
Juice of 1/2 lemon
1/2 teaspoon ground cumin
10 turns freshly ground black pepper
3 cups prewashed bagged spinach leaves
2 15-ounce cans white beans, drained and rinsed
2 small red peppers, , roasted and peeled or an equal amount from
    a 12-ounce jar of roasted red peppers, diced chopped
10 Kalamata olives, finely chopped
Salt, to taste

1. Combine the oil, lemon, cumin, and pepper in a medium bowl. Add the spinach leaves and toss.
2. Add the beans, red peppers, and olives. Toss again. Check and adjust seasonings.

Total time: 10 minutes
Serves 6 as a side salad

CANNELLINI BEAN, AVOCADO, AND TOMATO SALAD

This recipe is great at a meal with vegetarians (protein, fat, and simplicity), or at a party, and it easily doubles. It can be made in advance, except for the avocado, which should be added at the last minute.

2 cups cannellini beans (1 15-ounce can, drained and rinsed)
1/2 cup finely chopped red onion
1 1/2 tablespoons chopped basil
1 1/2 tablespoons chopped parsley
Grated zest of 1 lemon
2 cups cherry tomatoes, halved if they are large
2 tablespoons lemon juice
1 avocado
2 tablespoons extra virgin olive oil
Salt and pepper, to taste

1. Combine first 5 ingredients in a large bowl and toss. Add tomatoes and toss again.
2. Just before serving, peel and cut the avocado into cubes, sprinkle with lemon juice, and add to the salad.
3. Add olive oil, salt and pepper to taste, and toss again.

Total time: 10 minutes
Serves 4

BEAN AND CORN SALAD

This salad will keep for a week in your refrigerator. It's perfect for picnics, meals served when all your appliances are broken or being remodeled, or late nights at the office. In my house we often serve it on a bed of lettuce. If you plan right, all the ingredients will be in the house and you can make it at the last minute, in one bowl.

1 15-ounce can black, red, or white beans, drained and rinsed
1 15-ounce can corn, drained
1 red or green pepper (or a combination), diced
3 tablespoons finely diced red onion
2 tablespoons lime juice
1 teaspoon sugar
Dash of cayenne pepper
1/2 teaspoon cumin
1/2 teaspoon salt
2 tablespoons extra virgin olive oil
1/4 cup chopped cilantro leaves

1. Combine first 4 ingredients in a large bowl.
2. Combine all the other ingredients except cilantro in a small bowl to make salad dressing.
3. Pour salad dressing over beans and corn. Sprinkle with cilantro and toss.

Total time: 10 minutes
Serves 4

WILD RICE AND SMOKED CHICKEN SALAD

At a Buddhist potluck wedding, my carniverous oldest daughter figured what all smart cooks figure—for a potluck, there's no better dish to bring than Wild Rice and Smoked Chicken Salad. She was sitting at a picnic table happily spooning squares of meat into her mouth when she overheard a woman commenting about the odd texture of the tofu in the wild rice salad. It took my daughter a moment to consider this statement before she realized that all the other potluck dishes were meatless. Rushing to the table to remove the offending dish, she discovered it was too late—those vegetarian Buddhists had polished off the whole bowl.

1 1/2 cups dry wild rice
2 pounds whole smoked chicken or 1 pound smoked turkey meat
1/2 cup sundried tomatoes, cut into 1/4-inch strips
3/4 cup finely diced red onion
1/4 cup red wine vinegar
1/2 cup extra virgin olive oil
Salt and pepper, to taste
2 medium avocados
1 tablespoon lemon juice
1/4 cup minced parsley

1. Up to 24 hours ahead of time, cook the wild rice according to the package directions. Drain excess liquid and cool.
2. Cut chicken into bite-size pieces or cubes. Mix with the cooled rice. Stir in the sundried tomatoes and the onion.
3. Mix together the vinegar, oil, salt, and pepper in a small bowl or shake in a jar. Pour over salad and toss.
4. Just before serving, peel and cut the avocados into cubes, sprinkle with the lemon juice, and toss with the salad. Sprinkle with parsley.

Total time: 30 minutes. Cooking time: 60 minutes. Serves 12 at a buffet.

FARRO, TOMATO, AND MOZZARELLA SALAD

Here is a lazy quiz to see how much you've absorbed from the Lazy Gourmet: If you have to choose between two grains, one that cooks in 45 minutes and one that cooks in 15, and both Grain A and Grain B have the same texture and shape, which do you choose?

You choose 15-minute farro!

Farro is an Italian grain, very similar to its longer-cooking relation, barley. Both grains retain their individual shape after cooking. Both are great in soup, as a plain side, or in a salad. With farro, you should never be afraid to add half a cup of grated Parmesan after cooking. Farro is Italian. It does well with cheese.

This recipe can be done right before you serve it, but if you do it the lazy way, you'll follow each numbered instruction in advance and just throw the whole dish together in 5 minutes.

1/2 cup extra virgin olive oil
2 cloves garlic, peeled and finely chopped
1 1/2 teaspoons dried oregano
1/4 teaspoon red pepper flakes
1 1/2 teaspoons salt, divided
1 cup farro
3 tablespoons capers, rinsed
1/2 pound bocconcini (little balls of mozzarella), cut in half
1 1/2–2 cups cherry tomatoes (halved if large)
8 large leaves basil, torn into pieces
1/2 cup pitted Kalamata olives, halved
Freshly ground black pepper, to taste

1. In a small saucepan, heat oil over medium heat. Add garlic, oregano, and pepper flakes. Cook for 30 seconds. Take the pan off the heat and swirl it around. The garlic should be light brown, not really dark. Set the garlic mixture aside to cool to room temperature, at least 30 minutes or for as long as a day. I usually put it in a little jar and leave it out so the oil doesn't congeal.

2. Bring a 2-3-quart pot of water to a boil. Add 1 teaspoon salt to the water (reserve ¼ teaspoon salt for seasoning). Cook the farro for 15 minutes. Drain in a colander and rinse with cold water until farro is close to room temperature. Set aside. (If you're making the salad the next day, refrigerate the farro overnight.)

3. Toss mozzarella with cooled flavored oil and capers and let sit for up to 2 hours. Add farro, 1½ cups tomatoes, basil, and optional olives. Look at the salad to see if it needs more tomatoes for visual balance. Season with pepper and taste before adding remaining ¼ teaspoon salt (the capers and olives may add enough salt). Toss again.

Prep time: 45 minutes, divided
Resting time: 1 hour
Serves 6

CHICKEN SALAD WITH OLIVE VINAIGRETTE

I admit that I'm food processor-dependent. Who wants to spend all that time chopping when a whizzing blade can handle food demolition so easily? But if you're not an electronically oriented cook, don't worry. This recipe is only slightly less lazy when you do your own chopping and whisking.

Salad Dressing:
  2 large cloves garlic, peeled
  20 pitted Kalamata olives
  1 tablespoon mustard
  1/4 cup balsamic vinegar
  1/4 cup water
  2 teaspoons fresh thyme, plus more for garnish
  1/2 cup extra virgin olive oil
  Salt and pepper, to taste
Salad:
  1 head romaine lettuce, washed and torn into large pieces
  2-3 grilled chicken breasts, off the bone and cut into bite-size cubes or slices
  2 grilled red peppers, quartered
  Any other leftover cold vegetables, optional

1. Chop garlic in a small food processor. Add olives and chop. Add mustard, vinegar, water, thyme, and olive oil. Blend until combined and creamy. Taste before adding salt because the olives may be salty.
2. Put the lettuce in a bowl. Add the chicken, red peppers, and other optional vegetables. Toss with dressing. Garnish with thyme if desired.

Total time: 10 minutes
Serves 4 as a main course

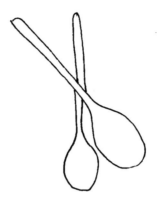

Soups

ALICE'S GAZPACHO
ASPARAGUS SOUP
ROASTED CARROT SOUP
RED LENTIL SOUP
CURRIED CAULIFLOWER SOUP
MUSHROOM SOUP
PEA SOUP
ROASTED TOMATO AND EGGPLANT SOUP
ROASTED BUTTERNUT SQUASH SOUP

The wonderful thing about soups is that all but the most tedious, unlazy ones can be made well in advance and served with two simple steps: heat and ladle into bowls. And some can even be served cold! Pair a nice soup with a big salad or with a sandwich and you've got a speedy, lazy meal that will put any of those 20-step gourmands to shame.

ALICE'S GAZPACHO

My cousin Alice is the epitome of relaxation in the kitchen. Whether preparing dinner for herself or for a dining room that has on occasion hosted diplomats and royalty, Alice serves the most delectable soups and stews, many of which can be thrown together in 10 minutes. After studying history for 50 years and teaching high school students to appreciate its lessons as she does, she understands that some things are worth spending time on (enjoying a meal with friends) and that some things are not (being chained to a stovetop). This gazpacho keeps well and is exactly what a hot day calls for. Serve it cold.

1 clove garlic
1/2 small onion, sliced
1/2 green pepper, sliced
3 ripe tomatoes, quartered
1 medium cucumber, peeled and sliced
1 teaspoon salt
Freshly ground black pepper, to taste
2 tablespoons extra virgin olive oil
1-3 tablespoons sherry vinegar, according to taste
1/2 cup chilled tomato juice, or V8, or water)
2 tablespoons chopped fresh dill or cilantro, divided

1. Chop garlic in food processor. Add onion and green pepper and chop. Add tomatoes and cucumber and pulse until roughly chopped.
2. Add salt and pepper, olive oil, sherry vinegar, and juice or water, and pulse. Add 1 tablespoon dill or cilantro and process until soup reaches desired consistency.
3. Serve cold, sprinkled with remaining dill or cilantro. Gazpacho keeps in the refrigerator for a day or two; after that it loses its freshness.

Total time: 10 minutes
Serves 4

ASPARAGUS SOUP

Nothing tastes or smells better than roasted asparagus and leeks. The inspiration for this recipe comes from Diane Rossen Worthington's book *Seriously Simple*. Her roasting technique also works well for other soups. Make this soup in advance for an elegant dinner party or serve for a light spring meal along with crusty French bread. It's good hot or cold.

2 1/2 pounds asparagus, woody ends broken off
2 leeks, white and light green part only
3 tablespoons extra virgin olive oil
Salt and freshly ground black pepper, to taste
3 1/2 cups chicken or vegetable stock
Plain yogurt and/or chopped herbs for garnish (optional)

1. Preheat oven to 425 degrees. Cut asparagus into 2-inch pieces. Cut leeks in half lengthwise and clean by running under cold water (sometimes leeks have dirt between their layers—very unappetizing). Roughly chop.
2. Place the asparagus, leeks, olive oil, and salt and pepper in a heavy roasting pan and toss to coat. Roast for 30-35 minutes, stirring from time to time. The leeks should be brown but not burnt.
3. Place half of the vegetable mixture in a blender, add 1½ cups of stock, and process until smooth, adding more stock if the mixture is too thick. Empty blender into a saucepan. Purée the remaining ingredients with 1½-2 cups more stock as needed. Add water if necessary. (This soup works best if you use the blender and not a food processor or an immersion blender, which do not produce the desirable smooth texture.)
4. Serve hot or cold, with or without garnish of yogurt and herbs.

Prep time: 10 minutes
Cooking time: 35 minutes
Serves 4

ROASTED CARROT SOUP

This recipe is in this book because nothing is easier and tastier than roasted carrots. Peel, toss with olive oil, and stick in the oven.

1 pound carrots, peeled and cut into 1-inch pieces (or baby carrots)
1 teaspoon salt, divided
1/4 teaspoon white pepper, divided
2 tablespoons extra virgin olive oil
3 tablespoons butter
1 medium onion, chopped
1 clove garlic, minced
1 half-inch piece ginger, peeled and minced
1 teaspoon ground cumin
1/2 teaspoon ground coriander
4 cups chicken or vegetable stock
1/4 cup orange juice
Plain yogurt, parsley, or cilantro for garnish

1. Preheat oven to 450 degrees. On a cookie sheet with a rim, toss carrots with ½ teaspoon salt, ⅛ teaspoon white pepper, and olive oil. Roast for 20 minutes, until browned.
2. While carrots roast, in a large saucepan over medium heat, melt the butter and sauté the onion for about 3 minutes, until softened. Add garlic and ginger. Continue cooking 2 mintues more. Add cumin and coriander and stir to combine.
3. Add roasted carrots and stock to the pot with the onions. Bring to a boil and cook uncovered 10 minutes.
4. Blend until smooth with an immersion blender or in a blender. Add orange juice. Thin with stock if necessary.
6. To serve, garnish with yogurt, parsley, or cilantro.

Total time: 30 minutes
Serves 4

RED LENTIL SOUP

Due to my Jewish suburban upbringing, it wasn't until law school that I had my first run-in with a lentil. Red lentils are the Lazy Gourmet's dream because they are small and delicate and don't have to be soaked. Still, you ought to rinse them under cold water and pick out any stones or deformed pieces before cooking them.

2 tablespoons extra virgin olive oil
2 medium onions, minced
1 1/2 teaspoon chili powder
1 teaspoon turmeric
Dash of cayenne pepper
1 tablespoon plus 1 teaspoon garam masala
2 tablespoons tomato paste
4 cups chicken or vegetable stock and 4 cups water
2 1/2 cups (1 pound) red lentils, rinsed
1 teaspoon salt
Juice of 1 lemon
Chopped parsley or cilantro for garnish

1. Heat oil in large saucepan and sauté onion over medium heat until it has browned slightly, about 5 minutes. While onion is sautéing, measure out the spices.
2. Add chili powder, turmeric, cayenne, garam masala, and tomato paste to the saucepan and sauté 2 more minutes.
3. Add stock-water combination and lentils. Bring to a boil, and then simmer 25 minutes, partly covered.
4. With an immersion blender, pulse the mixture 5 or 6 times (soup should not be too smooth). Add water if it is too thick, and salt and lemon juice to taste.
5. Garnish with parsley or cilantro if desired.

Prep time: 20 minutes. Cooking time: 30 minutes. Serves 4.

CURRIED CAULIFLOWER SOUP

After Mark's cholesterol took a climb for the worse, I banned cream and yolk-thickened sauces from my kitchen menu. But this soup has stayed in the mix because it is so simple and delicious. Besides what's a dollop (or three) of cream when distributed between two whole pounds of cauliflower?

2 tablespoons butter
1 onion, chopped
3 cloves garlic, minced (optional)
1-inch piece ginger, peeled and minced (optional)
2 1/2 teaspoons curry powder
1/2 teaspoon ground cumin
2-pound head of cauliflower, trimmed and sliced
4 cups chicken or vegetable stock
Salt and freshly ground black pepper
1 egg yolk
1/2 cup heavy cream
Chopped parsley or cilantro for garnish

1. Melt butter in a large soup pot. Sauté onion, garlic, and ginger in butter until soft. Add curry powder and cumin. Add cauliflower and stir to coat. Add stock, bring to a boil, lower the heat and cook 20 minutes, partly covered, until the cauliflower is soft, but not falling apart.
2. Purée, adding a bit more stock as necessary so that the soup purees smoothly. Taste for seasoning and add salt and pepper if necessary. (The soup can be prepared in advance up to this point, refrigerated for up to 3 days, and then reheated before proceeding.)
3. Just before serving, whisk together yolk and heavy cream in a small bowl. Drizzle ½ cup warm soup into yolk mixture so that egg doesn't cook and curdle, and then add mixture to soup. Serve garnished with minced parsley or cilantro.

Prep time: 15 minutes. Cooking time: 20 minutes. Serves 4.

MUSHROOM SOUP

My former French cooking teacher used to say (in French) that mushrooms without garlic aren't worth the fart of a rabbit. While that may frequently be the case, it is not true in the instance of this sherry-accented mushroom soup. The flavor is so rich and subtle that garlic would only overpower it. Chives or parsley sprinkled on top make a nice garnish.

3 tablespoons butter
2 onions, diced
2 pounds mushrooms, quartered or thickly sliced
2 tablespoons parsley, minced
1 tablespoon fresh thyme leaves
2 tablespoons good sherry
6 cups chicken or vegetable stock
Chopped chives or parsley, for garnish

1. In a medium saucepan, melt butter and sauté onions until soft. Add mushrooms and parsley and cook until the mushrooms give up their liquid and the liquid evaporates, around 5 minutes. Add thyme and sherry and cook until the sherry evaporates. Add stock, bring to a boil, and simmer 25 minutes.
2. Blend with immersion blender or in blender. Return soup to pot; adjust seasonings. The soup can be made in advance and reheated. Garnish with chives or parsley to serve.

Prep time: 30 minutes
Cooking time: 25 minutes
Serves 8

PEA SOUP

Although I always loved my job, coming home to my family was the highlight of my day. This soup developed because I never wanted to waste this precious time angsting over the stove. It takes almost no time and even less attention—perfect for any gourmet who wants to be anywhere but tied up in the kitchen.

3 cups chicken or vegetable stock
1 large shallot, minced
1 tablespoon extra virgin olive oil
20 ounces frozen peas
2 tablespoons grated Parmesan cheese

1. Heat stock to boiling on the stove or in the microwave.
2. In a medium saucepan with a lid, sauté shallot in oil until soft. Add frozen peas and stir.
3. Add hot stock to peas. Bring to a boil, cover, and cook at a simmer 5 to 10 minutes, or until peas are tender.
4. Carefully transfer soup to blender. Purée. Serve, or if you are feeling compulsive, strain soup to remove pea skins.
5. Serve with grated cheese.

Total time: 10–15 minutes
Serves 4

ROASTED TOMATO AND EGGPLANT SOUP

This is really a low-effort soup, because the tomatoes roast with no significant monitoring. After that, all the ingredients just meld together in the soup pot.

1 2-pound eggplant
8 roma tomatoes, cut in quarters
1 large red onion, cut in wedges
4 cloves garlic, peeled
2 tablespoons extra virgin olive oil
Salt and freshly ground black pepper, to taste
6 sprigs fresh thyme
4 cups chicken or vegetable stock
Minced parsley, for garnish

1. Preheat oven to 425 degrees.
2. Pierce eggplant all over (so it doesn't explode) and cook on a plate in microwave on high power for 10-15 minutes until soft. Cut in half lengthwise and let cool.
3. In a heavy roasting pan, toss together tomatoes, onion, garlic, oil, and salt and pepper. Roast 35 to 45 minutes, until the tomatoes have given up their liquid and are starting to brown.
4. Transfer tomatoes to a large soup pot. Scoop out the eggplant pulp from the skins and add to the pot. Add thyme and stock. Bring to a boil and then simmer for 15 minutes.
5. Purée with an immersion blender or in a blender. Adjust seasonings.
6. Garnish with parsley, if desired.

Prep time: 15 minutes
Cooking time: 1 hour
Serves 4-6

Roasted Butternut Squash Soup

This soup is a little more work than the others, due to the fact that you must pre-cook the squash. Double the recipe and call it an investment. You'll be glad you did.

1 1 1/2–2 pound butternut squash
2 tablespoons vegetable oil
1 onion, chopped
1 carrot, chopped
1 stalk celery, chopped
6 cups vegetable stock
Salt and freshly ground black pepper
2 tablespoons butter
1/2 cup fresh sage leaves

1. Preheat oven to 375 degrees. Cut squash in half lengthwise and scrape out the seeds. Pour ⅓ cup of water into a rimmed cookie sheet and place squash cut side down on the cookie sheet. Roast for 45 minutes. Let squash cool, and then scoop out the flesh.
2. In a deep saucepan, heat oil and sauté onion, carrot, and celery until onion is translucent. Add the cooked squash and cook, stirring from time to time, for 10 minutes. Add stock, bring to a boil, and simmer 20 minutes.
3. Puree with immersion blender or in a blender. Add more stock if necessary. Add salt and pepper to taste.
4. Melt butter and sauté the sage until crisp. Serve sage leaves on top of the soup.

Prep time: 20 minutes
Cooking time: 45 minutes (for squash), 30 minutes (for soup)
Serves 8

Vegetables and Sides

ROASTED ASPARAGUS
PAN-FRIED ASPARAGUS
STEAMED ARTICHOKES
ROASTED RED PEPPER SAUCE FOR ARTICHOKES
STEAMED BROCCOLI WITH CHEDDAR CHEESE
BROCCOLI PUREE
SPICY BROCCOLI
ROASTED BRUSSELS SPROUTS
SAUTÉED BRUSSELS SPROUTS
ROASTED CAULIFLOWER
CAULIFLOWER PURÉE
STEAMED EDAMAME
PAN-STEAMED GREEN BEANS
SAUTÉED SPINACH WITH GARLIC
SPICY CREAMED SPINACH
BAKED ACORN SQUASH
ZUCCHINI WITH PARMESAN
OVEN-ROASTED RATATOUILLE
ROASTED NEW POTATOES
EASY POTATO GRATIN
MASHED POTATOES

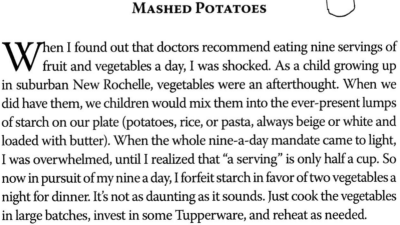

When I found out that doctors recommend eating nine servings of fruit and vegetables a day, I was shocked. As a child growing up in suburban New Rochelle, vegetables were an afterthought. When we did have them, we children would mix them into the ever-present lumps of starch on our plate (potatoes, rice, or pasta, always beige or white and loaded with butter). When the whole nine-a-day mandate came to light, I was overwhelmed, until I realized that "a serving" is only half a cup. So now in pursuit of my nine a day, I forfeit starch in favor of two vegetables a night for dinner. It's not as daunting as it sounds. Just cook the vegetables in large batches, invest in some Tupperware, and reheat as needed.

ROASTED ASPARAGUS

I don't even use my knife when cooking asparagus. That's how lazy this vegetable is. Just hold each asparagus stalk with one hand halfway down the stem, in between the tender tip and the blunt end of the stem, and the hand other on the blunt end of the stem, and bend until the stalk breaks. It will break naturally just above the tough, inedible part of the stem.

1 pound asparagus
2 tablespoons extra virgin olive oil
Salt and freshly ground black pepper
Parmesan cheese (optional)

1. Preheat oven to 425 degrees.
2. Break off ends of asparagus. Place on rimmed cookie sheet or roasting pan.
3. Drizzle with oil. Sprinkle with salt and pepper.
4. Roast in oven for 5 to 10 minutes, depending on thickness. Or grill the asparagus on an outdoor grill over medium-high heat for about 4 minutes, turning every 2 minutes. You don't want them to get too soft.
5. You can sprinkle grated or peeled strips of Parmesan on the asparagus, if you want, but it's fabulous plain as well.

Prep time: 5 minutes
Cooking time: 5-10 minutes, depending on thickness of asparagus
Serves 4

PAN-FRIED ASPARAGUS

Asparagus is so tender that it will cook in a flash. My daughters used to eat just the tips—the most delicate part—leaving their father (aka "Garbage Mouth") the stems (which are also delicious to those who are over the age of seven).

1 pound asparagus
2 tablespoons butter
Salt and freshly ground black pepper
Juice from half of a lemon

1. Break off ends of asparagus.
2. Melt the butter in a heavy skillet large enough to hold all the asparagus in single layer.
3. When the butter is melted, add the asparagus, turn the heat to medium, add salt and pepper, and cook until asparagus is browned slightly on all sides, around 5-7 minutes. Turn down heat and cook until just tender, about 2 minutes. Squeeze lemon juice over asparagus and serve.

Total time: 10 minutes
Serves 4

STEAMED ARTICHOKES

Lazy to cook, but not lazy to eat: that's the beauty of the artichoke. Eating one whole is a great way to slow down even the fastest chow hounds among us. My family members are all speedy eaters—except my daughter Molly. My heart broke just a little bit when she told me that one of her most vivid memories from childhood is sitting at our kitchen table, still eating her dinner, with Mark sponging off the table around her. Molly, this recipe is for you.

4 large artichokes
1 lemon
1/4 cup mayonnaise
1 teaspoon curry powder

1. Put a couple of inches of water in a large covered pot (choose one that will fit all the artichokes) and bring to a boil.
2. Cut the bottoms off the artichokes. Cut the lemon in half and rub one half on the cut ends of the artichokes. Place artichokes in boiling water, cut side down, cover, turn down the heat to a simmer, and cook until done, usually around 45 minutes. You know it's done when the leaves pull off easily.
3. While artichokes cook, mix together mayonnaise, curry powder, and 1 tablespoon lemon juice for sauce. Add more lemon if it seems too bland.
4. Remove the artichokes from the pot with a slotted spoon. Serve hot, warm, or cold.

To eat, pull off the leaves from the artichoke. Dip the flat ends of the leaves in the sauce and scrape the meat off with your teeth. When you get to the heart, cut away the thin leaves, scoop out the thistle, and eat the heart with the sauce.

Prep time: 5 minutes
Cooking time: 45 minutes
Serves 4

ARTICHOKES AND ROASTED RED PEPPER SAUCE

There are dozens of interesting sauces for artichokes. Melted butter with lemon is a classic. Also good are Cauliflower Purée (surprising, I know—page 58) and this roasted pepper sauce. If roasted peppers from a jar taste okay to you, you can skip the part of the recipe that calls for roasting the red peppers.

3 red peppers, roasted, peeled, seeded, and quartered, or 1 1/2
    cup roasted pepper from a jar
2 tablespoons extra virgin olive oil
1/4 small onion, thinly sliced
1 clove garlic, peeled, sliced thinly
4-6 basil leaves
Salt and freshly ground black pepper
1/2 cup vegetable or chicken stock

1. Heat oil in small saucepan and add onion and quartered peppers. Sauté for 5 minutes. Add garlic, basil, salt and pepper, and sauté for 1 minute. Add stock and turn heat to low. Cook 15 minutes until liquid has evaporated a little.
2. Blend mixture in blender. It should form a thick sauce. Taste and adjust seasoning.

Total time: 60 minutes
Makes 2 cups

STEAMED BROCCOLI WITH CHEDDAR CHEESE

When I had cancer, I read all the food-as-anti-cancer-weaponry books that I could get my hands on. Broccoli appeared again and again and I started getting pretty creative with it (lazy style) so that Mark wouldn't fuss too much about seeing it almost every night on the dinner plate. But there's nothing like the classic broccoli and cheddar cheese. I keep grated cheese in the fridge, we use it so often. You can substitute Monterey Jack, or, better yet, pepper jack.

1 pound broccoli (with stems or just the crown)
Grated cheddar cheese, to taste

1. Peel and cut the broccoli stems into ⅓-inch slices, on the diagonal. Cut off the florets. Or use just the crown and cut it into florets.
2. Steam broccoli for 7-10 minutes, until crisp-tender. Place in a bowl and sprinkle with grated cheddar cheese.

Total time: 20 minutes
Serves 4

BROCCOLI PUREE

We called this broccoli mush when the kids were growing up, and they loved it. Despite the title, I don't think they ever realized there was actual broccoli in it. *Green Eggs and Ham* was a big book in their day, so why not green mashed potatoes?

2 pounds broccoli with stems
1/2 teaspoon nutmeg (optional)
2 tablespoons butter
Salt and freshly ground black pepper

1. Peel the broccoli stems and cut them into ⅓-inch slices. Cut the rest of the broccoli into florets.
2. Steam broccoli for 7-10 minutes. (It should be still green but able to be pierced easily with a fork.)
3. Place broccoli in food processor and process. Add butter, nutmeg, and salt and pepper, and process to form puree. If it doesn't get smooth, add a little milk, sour cream, or yogurt. Adjust seasonings.

Total time: 20 minutes
Serves 4

SPICY BROCCOLI

I'm a good cook. I spent years of my adult life preparing delicious meals for my kids. But when you ask them now what dish they remember most from childhood, they'll tell you about Enchanted Broccoli Forest. And then they'll make a horrible face. To set the record straight, I made Enchanted Broccoli Forest only twice. Both times, Josie managed to trade Molly her "insides" of the dish—a very nice casserole made with rice and egg, for Molly's "outsides" (i.e. broccoli), a trade which I later learned both girls considered to be the lesser of two serious evils. This next recipe is nothing like Enchanted Broccoli Forest (which I thought was delicious). Enjoy.

1 pound broccoli, with stems
1 tablespoon extra virgin olive oil
1/4 teaspoon red pepper flakes
Salt, to taste

1. Peel the broccoli stems and cut them into ⅓-inch slices, on the diagonal. Cut the rest of the broccoli into florets.
2. Heat olive oil in a sauté pan with a lid. Add the broccoli slices and red pepper flakes and cook over high heat for 2-3 minutes, until broccoli is slightly browned. Lower the heat, add the florets, and cook 1 minute. Add ⅓ cup water. Cover and cook for 4 minutes, or until steam stops coming out of pan. Add salt.

Total time: 20 minutes
Serves 4

ROASTED BRUSSELS SPROUTS

This is another recipe where the taste is salty and crunchy. If it weren't so good for you, it would be decadent.

1 1/2 pounds Brussels sprouts
2 tablespoons extra virgin olive oil
Salt and freshly ground black pepper

1. Preheat the oven to 425 degrees.
2. Cut the very end off of the sprouts and then cut them in half lengthwise. Place them in a bowl and toss with olive oil, salt, and pepper. Include the leaves that fall off.
3. Put the sprouts on a rimmed cookie sheet. If you have time, turn them so the flat side is down. Roast for 20 minutes. You can toss them around after 15 minutes. The loose leaves will get crisp—watch that they don't burn.

These are great plain, but for even more flavor, you can toss the roasted sprouts with sage sautéed in brown butter.

Prep time: 5 minutes
Roasting time: 20 minutes
Serves 4

SAUTÉED BRUSSELS SPROUTS

We invented this recipe one Thanksgiving when we were looking for another vegetable dish but had no more oven space to bake, re-heat, or keep things warm. Easy to make quickly and last-minute, this fit the bill, and was delicious besides.

3 tablespoons butter
2 shallots, minced
12 sage leaves, chopped
1 pound Brussels sprouts, thinly sliced from the top down (discard the root end)
Salt and freshly ground black pepper, to taste

1. In a large sauté pan, over medium-high heat, melt butter until it just starts to brown. Add shallots and chopped sage leaves and cook until shallots start to soften.
2. Add the Brussels sprouts and cook for 5 minutes, until sprouts soften.
3. Add salt and pepper to taste.

Total time: 20 minutes
Serves 4

ROASTED CAULIFLOWER

This recipe is absolutely amazing. I first read about this method of cooking cauliflower in the *New York Times* but I've made it so often since then that I must own it by now. The roasting caramelizes the cauliflower, and the result is that this otherwise potentially bland veggie ends up tasting like salty candy. I am not a calorie counter by nature, but cauliflower has almost no calories and, as an added bonus, is supposed to protect against cancer. In the interest of full disclosure, it takes a few minutes to cut the cauliflower, but if you make it a lot, you'll get faster at doing it. Sometimes being lazy takes practice to perfect.

1 head of cauliflower
2-3 tablespoons extra virgin olive oil
Salt and freshly ground black pepper

1. Preheat oven to 425 degrees.
2. Cut the heavy stem and leaves off the cauliflower and discard. Cut the head of cauliflower in half lengthwise. Place the halves cut sides down, and cut into ⅓-inch slices, breaking slices up into 1-2-inch pieces. (Or cut into evenly sized florets with longish stems, discarding the rest or reserving for puree (see Cauliflower Purée, page 58).)
3. Place the cauliflower in a large bowl and toss with oil and salt and pepper. Place on a large rimmed cookie sheet.
4. Roast cauliflower for 25-30 minutes or until brown edges form. You can toss it around on the cookie pan 15 or 20 minutes into cooking, but it works even without this step.

Prep time: 5-10 minutes
Cooking time: 25-35 minutes
Serves 4 (or sometimes 2)

Cauliflower Purée

A good trick-the-children recipe is Cauliflower Purée. It looks just like mashed potatoes, but tastes sweet, not like steamed cauliflower at all!

1 head cauliflower
2 tablespoons butter
Salt and freshly ground black pepper
Nutmeg (optional)

1. Cut the heavy stem and leaves off the cauliflower and discard. Slice the cauliflower in half lengthwise and then into ½-inch slices. Place in a steamer and steam until soft, usually around 10 minutes.
2. Place hot cauliflower in food processor. Add butter, salt, and pepper. Puree. If it doesn't get smooth, pour in some milk or cream (but don't add too much—cauliflower has a lot of water in it and it easily becomes too watery).
3. Check for seasonings, and add nutmeg if desired.

Prep time: 10 minutes
Cooking time: 10 minutes
Serves 3-4

STEAMED EDAMAME

Ten years ago you could only get edamame in Japanese restaurants. But now these soy pods are all the rage. I love it when obscure foods go mainstream—although, to be fair, edamame was never an obscure food in Japan. It is probably the only appetizer snack that packs a protein punch without the aid of cheese or a sugary dipping sauce. That's the beauty of soy: it's all nutrition, all the time. Look for edamame in bags in the frozen vegetable section of your grocery store. Bet you can't eat just one.

1-pound bag whole edamame pods
Salt, to taste

1. Steam or boil frozen beans as per the package instructions.
2. Place in bowl and sprinkle with salt.

Eat the edamame by biting down on the pod, which pops out the beans. Eat the beans and discard the pod.

Total time: 10 minutes
Serves 4 as a side dish
Serves 8 as an appetizer

PAN-STEAMED GREEN BEANS

When I told one of my daughters that the cooking technique for these green beans was developed by Pam Anderson, she told me she always thought a chest that big would get in the way of cooking. No, not that Pam Anderson—I meant Pam Anderson the cookbook author.

One-pot cooking always qualifies as a lazy technique in my book, but beware, overcooked green beans are nobody's friend. So set your timer and when in doubt, undercook and get that pan off the heat ASAP.

1 pound green beans, stem end trimmed (you can sometimes buy
    them already trimmed at Trader Joe's or Costco)
4 teaspoons butter, divided
1/2 teaspoon salt
Freshly ground black pepper

1. If your beans are on the larger size, cut them in half (smaller beans and French beans can be left whole).
2. Place the beans in a saucepan 8 or 9 inches in diameter. Add ¼ cup to ⅓ cup water. The amount varies with the size of the pan, so you'll need to experiment a little.
3. Add 2 teaspoons of butter and the salt. Cook over medium heat until the water boils (this takes a minute or so).
4. Turn heat down, cover the pan, and cook for 5 minutes longer. Set a timer if you need it. Remove the lid and test. They should be crisp-tender. If they are done but there is still water in the pot, cook a little longer with top off to evaporate water and sauté beans a bit. Watch them carefully or the butter will burn.
5. Remove from heat. Toss beans with remaining butter and pepper.

Total time: 15 minutes
Serves 3-4

SAUTÉED SPINACH WITH GARLIC

There is nothing wrong with buying greens in a bag, especially when it comes to spinach. Compared to bunched spinach with those long, dirt-clinging stems, bagged spinach is a breeze to deal with (although you really should break off any thick stems you see for the purposes of this recipe), and baby spinach has almost no stems to speak of. With a recipe like this, you can make steakhouse-quality wilted spinach in the blink of a lazy eye.

2 tablespoons extra virgin olive oil
4 cloves garlic, peeled and thinly sliced
1 to 2 anchovies, minced, or 1/2 tablespoon anchovy paste (optional)
2-pound bag pre-washed baby spinach
Salt and freshly ground black pepper

1. Use a large deep sauté pan or stock pot with a thick bottom. Heat the pan until warm—but not too hot or the garlic will burn. Add the oil and garlic and sauté for 30 seconds. Add the anchovies, if using, and sauté 30 seconds.
2. Add the spinach with a pair of tongs, in large clumps. After each clump, toss the spinach around to coat with the oil. Repeat until all the spinach is added. Cook spinach uncovered, turning frequently, or cover the pan, turn the heat to low, and cook 2-4 minutes, tossing once. The spinach should be wilted. Toss once more and add salt and pepper.

Total time: 10 minutes
Serves 4

SPICY CREAMED SPINACH

The inspiration for this recipe comes from the late great author Laurie Colwin. If you haven't read her book *Home Cooking,* go to the bookstore now. Laurie Colwin was the first to write about home cooking in a fun, simple way. Josie and I have spent some time with this recipe and have tweaked it slightly from Laurie's original.

2 1-pound bags frozen spinach, defrosted
3 tablespoons butter
2 tablespoons minced onion
1 clove garlic, minced
2 tablespoons flour
3/4 cup vegetable or chicken stock
3/4 teaspoon celery salt
Freshly ground black pepper to taste
4 ounces pepper jack cheese, cut into 3/4-inch cubes

1. Put spinach in strainer. Press out excess liquid.
2. Preheat oven to 300 degrees and grease (butter, oil, or spray) a 1-quart casserole dish.
3. In a medium sized saucepan over medium heat, melt butter, sauté onion in butter until it begins to soften. Add garlic and cook 30 seconds. Add flour and cook 2 minutes. Add stock and cook until thickened, 1 or 2 minutes. Add celery salt and pepper. Add drained spinach and stir until well combined with sauce. Add jack cheese and stir until the cheese has started to melt.
4. Pour mixture into the prepared dish and bake uncovered for 45 minutes. Serve warm.

Prep time: 15 minutes
Baking time: 45 minutes
Serves 6-8

BAKED ACORN SQUASH

There's nothing more daunting for a novice cook than a hard-shelled squash. You can't bite into it without chipping a tooth; you can't peek inside to see what you'll actually be eating. And you can't eat it at all without applying high heat for a significant amount of time. But the fact is, cooking squash is absurdly lazy. Just slice it open, rub it with some seasonings, and abandon it to the oven while you put your feet up.

2 acorn squash
Salt and freshly ground black pepper
Extra virgin olive oil for coating the squash
2 tablespoons butter, divided
4 tablespoons maple syrup, divided

1. Preheat oven to 350 degrees.
2. Cut each squash in half with a large knife. Remove the seeds with a spoon or a melon baller. Rub cut sides of squash with olive oil and sprinkle with salt and pepper. Place cut side down on a rimmed cookie sheet.
3. Bake 30 minutes. Remove squash from oven, and turn the squash over so the cut side is up. In each squash half, place ½ tablespoon butter and 1 tablespoon maple syrup. (The recipe can be made in advance to this point and left out for 1 hour or so before final baking.)
4. Place squash in oven for 5 minutes to melt the butter. Serve warm.

Prep time: 5 minutes
Cooking time: 35 minutes
Serves 4

ZUCCHINI WITH PARMESAN

There's no way I can take credit for this recipe. It is simply an intuitive blend of flavors—tender zucchini, salty Parmesan, and pepper for bite. I never understood those cooks who made zucchini bread out of such a delightful green squash—it hides all the flavor of the produce. And is baking something the lazy gourmet has time for? Not this Lazy Gourmet, that's for sure.

1 pound small zucchini, trimmed
Salt and freshly ground black pepper
Parmesan cheese, grated

1. Cut zucchini into ⅓-½ inch circles or into quarters lengthwise and then cut each quarter into thirds, making 2-inch pieces.
2. Steam 5-7 minutes. Place in a serving bowl and toss with salt, pepper, and grated Parmesan.

Total time: 12 minutes
Serves 4

OVEN-ROASTED RATATOUILLE

Ratatouille is a French vegetable stew. The classic version requires sautéing each vegetable separately, which can take hours. But in the lazy gourmet version, the vegetables are baked instead of sautéed. Talk about a terrific shortcut. As for chopping, it can be as uneven as your lazy soul wants.

2 red onions, each cut in eight wedges lengthwise
1 1/2 pound eggplant, cut in 1 1/2-inch pieces
6 zucchini, trimmed, cut in half lengthwise, and then into 1 1/2-inch pieces
2 large red or green peppers, seeded and cut into 1 1/2-inch pieces
4-5 tablespoons olive extra virgin oil, divided
Salt and freshly ground black pepper
2 cups cherry tomatoes
3 cloves garlic, minced
2 teaspoons dried oregano
1/8 teaspoon red pepper flakes
2 tablespoons basil, cut in chiffonade
1 tablespoon balsamic vinegar

1. Preheat oven to 400 degrees. In a large bowl combine the onions, eggplant, zucchini and peppers. Toss with 3-4 tablespoons olive oil, and salt and pepper. Turn onto 2 large rimmed cookie sheets or roasting pans (you want the vegetables to have some space so they roast and don't steam). Roast for 30 minutes, tossing once or twice. Remove from oven.
2. In the same large bowl, toss the tomatoes with the garlic, remaining olive oil, salt and pepper, oregano, and red pepper flakes. Add to the eggplant mixture, toss and roast for 10 more minutes. Remove from oven.
3. Add the basil and balsamic, and toss to combine. Serve warm or at room temperature.

Prep time: 15 minutes. Cooking time: 45 minutes. Serves 4.

ROASTED NEW POTATOES

This is another one of those lazy recipes that leaves plenty of room for bending the rules. Toss potatoes with some sort of fat, season with spices, dried herbs, or whatever you have on hand that will hold up under additional heat, and roast as directed.

1 pound new or small Yukon Gold potatoes, halved
2 tablespoons extra virgin olive oil
1 teaspoon salt
10 turns freshly ground black pepper

1. Put a roasting pan big enough to hold all the potatoes in the oven, and preheat oven to 450 degrees.
2. In a bowl, toss the potatoes with olive oil, salt and pepper.
3. Put potatoes in hot roasting pan. Roast for 30 minutes, stirring once halfway through.

Total time: 30 minutes
Serves 4

EASY POTATO GRATIN

Next time you haul out the potatoes, banish the Americanized deep fryer and think European. Baked cheesy potatoes are a classic French staple known as a gratin. Since most gratin recipes call for time-consuming layering, normal gratins are not lazy. But once you get past the thin-slice knife work, this recipe is quick, easy and uses only a smidgen of cream (which ups the health factor, if only by just a bit).

1 clove garlic, cut in half
Vegetable oil for coating baking dish
2 pounds russet potatoes (about 3 potatoes)
2 1/4 cups milk
1/4 cup heavy cream
4 ounces grated Gruyere cheese (around 1 1/2 cups)
1 teaspoon salt, or to taste
15 turns freshly ground pepper, or to taste

1. Preheat the oven to 375 degrees. Rub a 13 x 9-inch baking dish with the garlic and spray with cooking spray or rub with oil. Set aside.
2. Peel the potatoes and slice them very thinly. I use the food processor for this.
3. Put the potatoes in a large bowl and add the milk, cream, 1 cup of the cheese, and salt and pepper. Toss until well mixed.
4. Using a slotted spoon, spoon the potatoes into the prepared baking dish and spread them evenly. Pour the remaining liquid and cheese over the potatoes. Sprinkle the top with the ½ cup of cheese.
5. Bake on a center shelf in the oven for 1 hour and 15 minutes, until it is nicely browned on top.

Prep time: 15 minutes
Baking time: 1 hour 15 minutes
Serves 4–6

MASHED POTATOES

Although mashed potatoes are not hard to make, the lazy gourmet only makes these for special occasions due to all the peeling, cooking, draining, and mashing required. Josie suggests you double-batch them and mix the leftovers with an egg or two and your favorite spices, and fry them up as potato cakes. This doesn't sound lazy to me, but I'll give it to her for an innovative use of leftovers.

3 pounds russet potatoes, peeled and cut into 2-inch pieces
1 cup milk
1/4 cup heavy cream
2 tablespoons butter
2 teaspoons of salt, divided
Freshly ground black pepper, to taste

1. Place the potatoes in a large pot and cover with cold salted water. Bring to a boil and cook for 20 minutes until the potatoes can be pierced with a fork.
2. While potatoes cook, in a small saucepan, heat milk, cream, and butter with ½ teaspoon of salt and and a few turns of pepper.
3. Drain the potatoes and in the pot in which they cooked or in a large bowl, mash with ½ teaspoon salt. Add the milk-butter-cream mixture little by little and continue to mash until smooth. Taste to see if there is enough salt and butter.
4. At this point, the potatoes can be set aside and even refrigerated in a glass bowl. Reheat the potatoes in the microwave. If you do this, you may need to add more milk to preserve the smooth consistency.

Prep time: 15 minutes (peeling potatoes)
Cooking time: 25 minutes
Serves 6

Vegetarian Meals

Eggs
Pasta
Rice, Grains, and a Great Vegetarian Chili

It was an unpleasant shock for me when my children decided to become vegetarians. But over time I expanded my vegetarian options so that now I can whip together a meal that pleases both me and my remaining vegetarian child. (Josie reverted back to a carnivore lifestyle when she started at the Cornell Hotel School. Her darling husband Alex, however, recently embraced vegetarianism.)

The secret to pleasing vegetarians and meat-eaters alike is to combine several non-meat options to form a meal that doesn't feel like a scoop of Second Thought on a Plate. When I have vegetarians for dinner, I serve one or two vegetables, a grain, a salad, and some animal protein for those of us who eat it.

This chapter is not just about assembling a buffet of sides, although many of the recipes can be served with a meal featuring animal protein. It is about making meat-free meals—whether or not you abstain on principle or just according to mood.

Eggs

EGG SOUFFLÉ
CHILE EGG PUFF
SAVORY FRENCH TOAST WITH CHEESE
FEATHERED EGGS

Eggs make a fabulous lazy dinner because they are quick to put together and often don't require more than one bowl. An added lazy bonus is that eggs (and the ingredients that complement them) keep for a very long time in the refrigerator. This makes them the perfect to-hell-with-shopping dinner.

As testament to the extent of my laziness, I am not including omelets in this chapter. An omelet makes a great meal, requires only three eggs, a half a cup of leftovers and a little cheese, but also demands technique. Technique is not lazy.

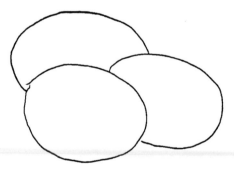

EGG SOUFFLÉ

To be honest, this is not truly a soufflé at all, but it puffs up like one. The ingredients are simply eggs, flour, and milk—the same ingredients that are in pancakes, crepes, popovers, or Dutch babies. Because this dish is extremely easy to make, and because these ingredients are easy to keep stocked, we eat egg soufflé on the evenings when we've gotten home late and there's nothing else edible in the fridge. Serve with a salad and call it a day.

2 tablespoons butter
1/2 cup all-purpose flour
1 teaspoon salt
4–5 turns freshly ground black pepper
3 eggs
1 cup milk

1. Preheat oven to 425 degrees. Place butter in a 1-quart soufflé dish and place dish on bottom rack of oven while oven is heating up.
2. Put flour, salt, and pepper in a medium bowl. Beat in eggs one at a time. (The mixture should be very thick at the beginning.) Add milk, a little at a time, beating constantly.
3. Remove soufflé dish from oven and rotate it to coat sides with melted butter. Pour egg mixture into dish and put it back in oven for 25 minutes, until it is puffed and brown around the edges. Serve immediately.

Prep time: 7 minutes
Baking time: 25 minutes
Serves 2 or 3

CHILE EGG PUFF

So you have company coming for breakfast, or teenagers coming for dinner, or too much cottage cheese in the house. This recipe is great because it has a dash of green, but the green is in the form of canned chilies, and those never go bad. A shortcut "prep" trick that I adore is to keep massive blocks of cheddar cheese in the house, grate them a half-pound at a time, and store in Tupperware. Josie says you can shortcut my shortcut by buying shredded cheese, but it's overpriced, and has a powdery sort of coating on it. Sometimes I wonder whose kitchen she grew up in.

2 tablespoons butter
5 eggs
1/4 cup all-purpose flour
1/2 teaspoon baking powder
1/4 teaspoon salt
8 ounces (1 cup) cottage cheese
1/4 lb. (1–2 cups) grated Monterey Jack and/or cheddar cheese
3 1/2 ounces diced green chilies (1 small can)

1. Preheat the oven to 350 degrees. Melt the butter in the microwave or in a small sauté pan over a very low flame.
2. In food processor combine eggs, flour, baking powder, salt, cottage cheese, grated cheese, and melted butter. Blend. Pulse in peppers.
3. Bake in greased pie plate or an 8 x 8-inch pan for 35 minutes until it is nicely browned on top.

Prep time: 10 minutes
Baking time: 35 minutes
Serves 4

SAVORY FRENCH TOAST WITH CHEESE

I first discovered this recipe in one of Mollie Katzen's recipe books and became so addicted that I made it once a week for about a year in the 1980s. When my eldest daughter was hired as a cook at a family camp kitchen in Yosemite, she made breakfast for 300 using this recipe. Diners poured maple syrup all over it, and complained that it tasted awful. She called me, beside herself. She hadn't realized that the rest of the world likes their French toast sweet, not savory.

3 eggs, lightly beaten
1 1/2 cup milk
1/2 teaspoon salt
Freshly ground black pepper (optional)
1 teaspoon dried basil, oregano, or thyme
1 pound stale challah or bread of your choice, cut into 8 1-inch
    slices
2 tablespoons butter
1/2 cup grated cheese (cheddar, swiss, or gouda)

1. Combine eggs, milk, salt, pepper and dried herbs in a large flat dish (a 9 x 13-inch baking dish is good). Soak bread on both sides for 5 minutes. You want it to absorb the egg mixture. If there's not enough egg mixture, add more milk.
2. Melt the butter in a large sauté pan. In batches, sauté the soaked bread until it is browned on the bottom. Flip and sprinkle with 2 tablespoons cheese. Cook until cheese is melted and the other side is browned.

Prep time: 10 minutes
Cooking time: 10 minutes
Serves 4

FEATHERED EGGS

I think the original name of this recipe was featherbed eggs, but I mispronounced it and we all call it feathered eggs now. Feathered Eggs is really just bread pudding, which is really just bread cooked in custard, which is really just bread cooked in beaten egg. Play around with the ingredients, and feel free to use cubed bread instead of slices. This is a very flexible little recipe. I always make it when we rent a vacation house with lots of friends at Sea Ranch, because it's so easy to prepare. I'm even lazier on vacation than in real life. I prepare the dish the night before and bake it in the morning.

6–8 slices challah-type bread, sliced 1 inch thick
1 1/2 cups grated sharp cheddar cheese (or any melting cheese)
6 eggs
1 1/2 cups milk
1 teaspoon dried basil
Salt and freshly ground black pepper, to taste

1. Preheat the oven to 350 degrees.
2. Grease a 9 x 13-inch baking dish. Place the bread in the dish in a single layer. Sprinkle the bread with the cheese.
3. Beat the eggs slightly in a bowl and beat in the milk, basil, salt, and pepper. Pour over the bread and cheese. Bake 45 minutes. (If not baking right away, you can cover the dish, refrigerate overnight, and in the morning place it in a cold oven turned to 350 degrees for 1 hour). When it's done it will be brown and puffy.
4. Let cool slightly before serving. To serve, cut into pieces.

Prep time: 10 minutes
Cooking time: 45 minutes
Serves 4–6

Pasta

PASTA ALLA CECCA
PENNE WITH SIMPLE BALSAMIC-TOMATO SAUCE
FAST MACARONI AND CHEESE
PASTA ALLA PUTTANESCA
PASTA SALAD WITH TOMATOES, BROCCOLI, AND CHEESE
ASIAN PEANUT-SESAME NOODLES
LARGE-BATCH VEGETARIAN SPAGHETTI SAUCE
LARGE-BATCH MACARONI AND CHEESE
PENNE CASSEROLE WITH TWO CHEESES

With all the delicious pesto and tomato sauces that you can buy in the grocery store, pasta as a main dish is almost too lazy to be true. In my heyday, I used to make both pesto and tomato sauce from scratch, but aside from the price break that comes from home cooking (which my more frugal daughter was quick to point out), there is really no reason not to buy your basic sauces at the market. You can always jazz them up with fresh garlic, fresh basil, or red pepper flakes. But if you're not into bottled or are just tired of bottled, try these (still lazy) meatless pasta dishes.

PASTA ALLA CECCA

I feel guilty calling this a recipe. It is more of a great idea: chop some tomatoes, toss with olive oil, garlic, basil and pepper flakes, dump everything on pasta and call it Italian. The only problem is that this recipe requires fresh wonderful tomatoes, so it really only works in summer and early fall. Better for its rarity? I think so.

5 large tomatoes (about 4 cups, diced)
1/3 cup extra virgin olive oil
1-3 cloves garlic, sliced very thin
1 cup basil leaves, julienned
1/4 teaspoon red pepper flakes
1 pound pasta (spaghetti is classic, but it works with any shape)
Salt and freshly ground black pepper

1. Seed and chop the tomatoes. Put in a large non-reactive bowl with olive oil, garlic, basil, pepper flakes, and salt and pepper. Let sit while the pasta is cooking (or several hours).
2. Cook pasta, following package directions. Drain pasta, place it in a large serving bowl, and pour the tomatoes over it.

Alternatives: Add one or several of the following ingredients to the sauce: 1-2 tablespoons balsamic vinegar, 8-10 pitted kalamata olives; 8-12 quartered sundried tomatoes; 2-4 tablespoons capers

Total time: 20 minutes
Serves 4

PENNE WITH SIMPLE BALSAMIC-TOMATO SAUCE

I never had boys in the house. Or so I thought, until my girls had a party that I only found out about because of a broken window. If I'd had sons instead of daughters, I imagine I would have had to cook in greater mass than I ever did. My friend Nancy adapted a Marcella Hazan recipe to cook for her son whenever he showed up unannounced with half his soccer team.

1 pound penne
1 tablespoon extra virgin olive oil
3-4 garlic cloves
2 sprigs fresh rosemary
1 28-ounce can whole peeled tomatoes, drained
Salt and freshly ground black pepper
2 teaspoons balsamic vinegar
Grated Parmesan cheese

1. In a large pot, bring water to boil for cooking the pasta. While the water is coming to a boil, peel garlic and slice very thinly.
2. When the water boils, add 1 teaspoon salt and then the penne and cook according to package directions.
3. While the pasta cooks, in a large saucepan heat olive oil and sauté garlic and rosemary until garlic sizzles. Add canned tomatoes (without juice). Break them up a little as they cook. Add salt and pepper and cook for 10-12 minutes. Discard the rosemary stalk.
4. When the pasta is done, reserve ½ cup of the cooking water. Drain the pasta and add to sauce. Turn heat to low and toss together for 2-3 minutes. Add some cooking water if the sauce seems dry.
5. Turn off heat. Add vinegar. Toss and serve with grated cheese.

Total time: 25 minutes
Serves 4

FAST MACARONI AND CHEESE

I do not like powdered cheese. It isn't a normal color and it doesn't have natural flavor. Even when it's organic, cheese should not be dehydrated. So put away those bright orange-lettered boxes and make macaroni the old-fashioned way. I promise, the steps remain the same: boiling water and stirring with a spoon. It helps if you keep some grated cheddar cheese in the refrigerator.

1 1/2 cups small elbow macaroni
3 tablespoons milk
2 tablespoons butter
6 turns freshly ground black pepper
1/2 teaspoon onion salt
1/2 teaspoon dry mustard
2 cups grated cheddar cheese, or more according to taste

1. Bring 3 cups of water to boil. Add macaroni and boil 4 minutes at high heat and 7 minutes at low, stirring from time to time. The water should evaporate. Turn off the heat. (If the water doesn't completely evaporate and the macaroni is cooked, drain the macaroni and put it back in the pan for the next step.)
2. Add milk, butter, pepper, onion salt, and dry mustard, and then the cheese. Stir until the butter and cheese melt.

Total time: 20 minutes
Serves 4

PASTA ALLA PUTTANESCA

I will not claim to own this recipe. Pasta puttanesca ("whore's pasta") might be as old as the profession itself. This is another one of those beautiful dishes that can be assembled using mostly imperishable ingredients.

1/3 cup extra virgin olive oil
8 cloves garlic, peeled
9 anchovies
1/4 teaspoon red pepper flakes
4 medium tomatoes, chopped and seeded or 1 28-ounce can
    tomatoes, drained and chopped
12 Kalamata olives, pitted and halved
2 teaspoons capers, drained
1 pound pasta, any shape
5 cloves garlic, peeled and minced
1/3 cup chopped parsley
2 tablespoons julienned basil
Grated Parmesan cheese

1. Put water on to boil for the pasta.
2. Heat olive oil in a large saucepan. Add 8 whole garlic cloves, and cook until they brown a little, about 2 minutes. Add the anchovies.
3. When the anchovies fall apart, add red pepper flakes, tomatoes, olives, and capers. Cook over medium heat for 30 minutes. (After tomatoes have cooked for 20 minutes, put pasta in boiling water to cook according to package directions.)
4. Add the chopped garlic, parsley, and basil to the tomatoes. Simmer 5 minutes.
5. When the pasta is cooked, toss with half the sauce, and place in a large serving bowl. Pour remaining sauce on top. Serve with grated Parmesan.

Prep time: 15. Cooking time: 30 minutes. Serves 4-6.

PASTA SALAD WITH TOMATOES, BROCCOLI, AND CHEESE

I couldn't resist throwing a little fish into this recipe. You can leave it out, but plenty of vegetarians these days look with forgiving eyes on the protein of the sea. Josie insists you can use 2 tins of high-quality drained canned tuna instead of fresh tuna in this recipe. I suppose she's right, but it's not quite as classy that way.

1 pound fusilli or penne pasta
8 ounces broccoli florets
2 tablespoons balsamic vinegar
2 tablespoons red wine vinegar
Salt and freshly ground black pepper
3/4 teaspoon dried oregano
3 tablespoons fresh basil, chopped
1/4 cup red onion, minced and rinsed with cold water
4 tablespoons extra virgin olive oil
3 medium tomatoes, cut in chunks
2 ounces cheddar, cubed
8 ounces grilled tuna, cubed (optional)

1. Cook pasta in salted water according to package directions. 2-3 minutes before pasta is finished, add broccoli. Drain pasta and broccoli, rinse with cold water, and drain again. Place in a large bowl.
2. Make dressing: combine vinegars with salt and pepper, and add oregano, basil, onion, and olive oil. Pour over pasta and broccoli and toss.
3. Add tomatoes and cheddar. Add tuna, if using, and toss again.

Total time: 30 minutes
Serves 4-6

ASIAN PEANUT-SESAME NOODLES

Death to delivery, that's what I call this dish. Forget overpriced Asian take-out. Forget those horrible white containers clogging up your refrigerator. Save some money and some time and get your Asian peanut sauce fix at home. It's better this way, I promise.

Josie's "hate to shop" tips: buy chopped ginger in a jar (Ginger People makes a good one) and use frozen broccoli florets (cooked) instead of cucumber.

1 inch peeled ginger (1 tablespoon, minced)
2 cloves garlic
2 tablespoons sesame oil
3 1/2 tablespoons soy sauce
2 tablespoons rice vinegar
3 tablespoon peanut butter (or combination equal amounts of peanut butter and Chinese sesame paste.)
1/2 tablespoon light brown sugar
1 teaspoon Chinese chili paste with garlic (Lan Chi brand)
1/2 pound Chinese egg noodles, fresh, or spaghettini
3 tablespoons chopped green onion
1/3 cup chopped cilantro
Half a peeled cucumber cubed or 2 cups cooked broccoli in small pieces

1. In a small food processor, mince garlic and ginger. Add sesame oil, soy sauce, rice vinegar, peanut butter and sesame paste, sugar, and chili-garlic paste. (Add a little water if mixture is too thick.) Set aside.
2. Cook Chinese noodles in boiling water for 5 minutes. Drain and rinse. Toss with sauce.
3. Add green onion, and cilantro and toss. Add cucumber or broccoli and toss again.

Total time: 15 minutes
Serves 2-3

LARGE-BATCH SPAGHETTI SAUCE

My children's Bubby gave this recipe to Mark when he left for college. My kids still don't believe that he ever made it. Their memory of him in the kitchen is standing over the sink washing dishes. But Bubby's tomato sauce got us through decades, with kids and without. Make it, jar it, and freeze it. The recipe yields 8 quarts of sauce. That's 16 pint jars, or, depending on your brand, $40-$100 worth of store-bought sauce. If you don't have a pot big enough to cook all of this at once, halve the recipe. You'll never buy bottled again.

1/4 cup extra virgin olive oil
4 stalks celery, cut in 1/4-inch slices*
6 carrots, peeled and sliced thinly*
4 medium onions, peeled and chopped*
6 cloves garlic, peeled and sliced
2 green peppers, seeded and chopped*
1 1/2 pounds mushrooms, sliced*
2 pounds ground turkey or beef (optional)
6 28-ounce cans whole Italian plum tomatoes, drained
24 ounces tomato paste
1-2 tablespoons dried basil
1-2 tablespoons dried thyme
1-2 tablespoons dried oregano
1-2 tablespoons dried rosemary, or 2 6-inch sprigs of fresh rosemary
4-6 bay leaves
1/2 cup chopped parsley
2 teaspoons salt
1/2 teaspoon freshly ground pepper
2 cups red wine

1. In a large soup pot, heat olive oil. Turn heat to medium-high and sauté celery, carrots, and onion 15 minutes. Add garlic and sauté 1 minute. Add green peppers and sauté 5 minutes. Add mushrooms and sauté until they release their liquid, about 5 minutes. (Add the meat, if using. Cook until it loses the raw look.)

2. Add tomatoes (break them up with a spoon as you add them), tomato paste, basil, thyme, oregano, rosemary, salt and pepper, and red wine. Stir well.

3. Bring to boil and then turn down heat to a simmer. Cook uncovered on low heat for 2 hours (or more if you want a thicker sauce). Stir occasionally to make sure the sauce doesn't stick to the bottom of the pot.

4. Taste and adjust seasonings. If the sauce is too acidic, add a teaspoon of sugar. Don't be afraid to add more herbs. The longer the sauce cooks, the sweeter it tastes.

*The onions, carrots, and celery can be chopped (pulsed) together in the food processor. You can also chop the green pepper and slice or roughly chop the mushrooms in the processor.

Prep time: 1 hour
Cooking time: 2–3 hours
Makes 8 quarts

LARGE-BATCH MACARONI AND CHEESE

The best thing about putting this collection of recipes together is that it gives me a chance to look at all my favorite recipes and know that some of them I don't ever have to eat again. Not that this isn't a killer recipe. It's just that my family ate a version of this every week for 15 years. That's 810 batches, maybe more. This macaroni and cheese keeps well in the freezer and can be transferred frozen to the oven in the morning. Program your oven to cook automatically so it's done when you get home from work. New parents—enjoy.

3 pounds elbow macaroni
1/2 pound butter
2 onions, minced
5 cubes vegetable or chicken bouillon
3/4 teaspoon white pepper
2 tablespoons plus 1 teaspoon dry mustard
1/4 teaspoon nutmeg
9 cups milk
1 1/3 cups flour
7 cups grated cheddar cheese

1. Put a very large pot of water on to boil (this will take a while). Add 1 teaspoon salt and cook the macaroni until al dente, 5-6 minutes. Don't overcook since it will bake again in the sauce. Drain and run cold water over noodles. Return to pot.
2. While the water is coming to a boil, in a large saucepan, melt the butter and sauté the onions until softened. Add the bouillon cubes and the pepper, dry mustard, and nutmeg.
3. While the onions cook, bring the milk to a simmer in a large saucepan. Don't let it boil.

4. Add the flour to the butter and onions. Let it cook a minute. Add the hot milk and whisk until well-combined and thickened. This can take 5 minutes or more, depending on how hot the milk is when it goes in. Turn off heat, and stir in 6 cups of the cheese until cheese melts.

5. Stir the cheese sauce into the drained noodles. Taste for seasoning (it may need more salt or pepper). Pour the mixture into 4 large greased foil casserole dishes. Sprinkle the remaining cheese over the casseroles, about ¼ cup on each.

6. Bake each casserole uncovered 25 minutes at 350 degrees. Or, if you are freezing the macaroni and cheese, let the casseroles cool and wrap well in foil.

7. To cook it right from the freezer using an oven timer, unwrap the casserole and place in the cold oven in the morning. Set the oven to turn on (to 350 degrees) one hour before you come home in the evening.

Prep time: 1 hour
Baking time: 25 minutes
Makes 4 casseroles
Each casserole serves 4

PENNE CASSEROLE WITH TWO CHEESES

This is a dish suited for company and is my go-to dish if I'm craving lasagna. It requires no layering (and is therefore lazy) but still bakes up bubbly like a lasagna should.

2 tablespoons extra virgin olive oil
2 medium onions, chopped
3 cloves garlic, minced
3 28-ounce cans Italian plum tomatoes, drained
1 1/2 tablespoons dried basil
1/2 teaspoon red pepper flakes
2 cups vegetable or chicken stock
Salt and freshly ground black pepper
1 pound penne
1/2 pound Havarti cheese, grated
1/2 cup pitted Kalamata olives
1/2 cup grated Parmesan cheese
2 tablespoons fresh basil, julienned

1. Preheat the oven to 375 degrees.
2. In a large saucepan, warm olive oil and sauté onion and garlic until soft. Add tomatoes, basil, and red pepper flakes and bring to a boil, breaking up tomatoes with the back of a wooden spoon. Add stock and bring to a boil. Reduce heat to medium and cook uncovered 1½ hours until it makes a chunky sauce. Season with salt and pepper.
3. In a large pasta pot, bring water to a boil and cook pasta according to directions until al dente. Drain. Return penne to the pot and toss with the Havarti cheese and tomato sauce. Transfer to a buttered 13 x 9-inch baking pan. Sprinkle the pasta with olives and Parmesan cheese. Bake 30 minutes, or until the top is browned. Sprinkle with basil, and serve immediately.

Prep time: 30 minutes. Cooking time: 2 hours. Serves 6.

Rice, Grains, and a Great Vegetarian Chili

RISOTTO WITH ASPARAGUS IN THE PRESSURE COOKER
PORCINI MUSHROOM RISOTTO IN THE PRESSURE COOKER
EASY VEGETARIAN CHILI
RISOTTO AL SALTO
FARRO AND ROASTED BUTTERNUT SQUASH
QUINOA PILAF
QUINOA PILAF WITH GARBANZO BEANS
ZUCCHINI COUSCOUS

What follows are not recipes for plain rice. These recipes are for those occasions when you want a substantial grain, or a grain combined with vegetables, or an easy vegetarian chili. Plain rice is nice, but Lazy Gourmet rice is a lifestyle.

RISOTTO WITH ASPARAGUS IN THE PRESSURE COOKER

I grew up believing that a pressure cooker was a dangerous weapon that could blow up and kill me at any moment. My mother and my friends' mothers made us leave the kitchen whenever they cooked with one. I never understood the risk when the results were so gloppy. But times they are a-changing. My neighbor Samantha taught me that pressure cookers are not only no longer dangerous, they are perfect for making creamy, cheesy, 7-minute risotto.

Traditional risotto cooks for at least 20 minutes and can't be left alone for a moment. You have to stir and add stock, and stir and add stock. Not only that, you have to keep the stock hot (which requires a second burner and a second pot). Distinctly not lazy. Enter the pressure cooker. You could easily substitute zucchini or frozen fava beans for the asparagus. Naturally, frozen anything is a Josie-idea. But this time it's really not a bad one.

3 cups vegetable or chicken stock
1 pound asparagus, washed, trimmed, and cut in 1-inch pieces
1 tablespoon extra virgin olive oil
1 large shallot or 1/2 onion, minced
1 1/2 cups Arborio rice
1/2 cup dry white wine
2/3 cup grated Parmesan cheese
Freshly ground black pepper

1. Bring stock to a boil in a saucepan. Add asparagus and simmer 3 minutes. Turn off the heat. Remove asparagus with a slotted spoon and set aside.
2. In pressure cooker, heat oil and sauté shallot or onion until it starts to soften. Add rice and stir until coated with oil. Add wine and bring to a boil and cook until it has evaporated. (The recipe can be made ahead to this point.)

3. Turn on the flame under the pressure cooker, add the stock, put on the cover, and raise the pressure. When steam comes out, turn the flame down to maintain an even pressure, and set the timer for 7 minutes. (The steam should still be coming out, but slowly and it should not be screeching. If it is making a lot of noise, the heat is too high.)

4. When the timer goes off, follow the manufacturer's directions for letting out the steam (be sure to face the steam away from you). When the steam has been released, open the cooker. There will be a layer of thick liquid on top. This is normal. Stir it into the rice, and then stir in the asparagus and cheese and season with pepper.

Prep time: 20 minutes
Cooking time: 10 minutes
Serves 6 as a side dish
Serves 4 as a main course

PORCINI MUSHROOM RISOTTO IN THE PRESSURE COOKER

I hang my head in shame. There is a bit more preparation in this recipe than would otherwise please the Lazy Gourmet. But you can do most of the preparation far in advance. In addition, this risotto is fancy enough to be not just dinner-party-worthy, but blow-away-dinner-party-worthy.

1 cup dried porcini mushrooms
1 cup vegetable or chicken stock
3 cups sliced crimini or white mushrooms, or a combination
2 tablespoons extra virgin olive oil, divided
1 clove garlic, peeled and minced
3 tablespoons minced parsley
1/2 cup finely minced shallots
1 1/2 cups arborio rice
1/2 cup dry white wine
1/2 cup grated Parmesan cheese

1. Soak the dried porcini in 2 cups warm water for 20 minutes. Strain through a paper towel, reserving the liquid. Rinse and chop and set aside. Add enough stock or water to the mushroom water to make 3 cups. Set aside.
2. In the pressure cooker pot, sauté the fresh mushrooms in 1 tablespoon olive oil over medium high heat. When mushrooms are soft, add the minced garlic and 1 tablespoon minced parsley. Set the rest of the parsley aside. Remove the cooked mushrooms to a small bowl.
3. In the pressure cooker (without washing it out), add the remaining tablespoon oil and sauté the minced shallots until soft. Add the rice and stir until coated with oil. Add the white wine and bring to a boil until the liquid evaporates, stirring the rice while you do so. Stir in the chopped porcini mushrooms. Turn off the heat.

4. Exactly 10 minutes before you want to eat, turn on the flame underneath the pressure cooker, add the mushroom water, put on the cover, and raise the pressure. When steam comes out, turn down the flame a little and set the timer for 7 minutes.

5. When the timer goes off, turn off the heat, let out the steam following the manufacture's directions. There will be a layer of thickened liquid on top. This is normal. Stir it into the rice and then stir in the cooked fresh mushrooms to let them heat up in the warm rice for a minute. Stir in the remaining parsley and the Parmesan cheese.

Prep time: 30 minutes
Soaking time: 30 minutes
Cooking time: 10 minutes
Serves 6 as a first course or side dish
Serves 4 as a main course

EASY VEGETARIAN CHILI

One of my culinary inspirations is the late food writer Laurie Colwin. Colwin wrote about preparing honest, deliciously straightforward food in her small apartment kitchen— on single burners, in a galley-style set up, with minimal ingredients. This recipe is based on one of Colwin's classics and it is a nonstop hit. It is best made in massive double batches (if you have the pot for it) and then frozen on top of plain brown rice so that it can be distributed to 1) New Parents, 2) Sick People, 3) Kids Living Away From Home, or 4) Yourself So You Don't Have to Cook When You Don't Feel Like It.

1 pound (2 cups) small dried beans (black, red, or a combination)
1 large onion, chopped
1 28-ounce can whole plum tomatoes, with juice
3 cups water
4 cloves garlic, peeled and minced
1 tablespoon chili powder
1 teaspoon ground cumin
1 tablespoon dried oregano
1 tablespoon dried basil
2 teaspoons salt
20 turns freshly ground black pepper

1. Pick over beans to remove dirt or stones, and rinse. In a heavy-bottomed 4-quart casserole dish or Dutch oven (enameled cast iron is good), place beans, onion, tomatoes, and water (a trick: 3 cups of water is the same as the empty tomato can). Bring to boil, cover, reduce heat to a low simmer, and simmer around 3½ hours, stirring from time to time so beans don't stick.
2. Remove the cover. Add garlic, chili powder, cumin, oregano, basil, and salt and pepper. Stir and cook, uncovered, 30 minutes. Check seasonings and adjust if necessary.

Serve with brown rice and garnish with olives, cheddar cheese, diced tomato, cilantro, and green onions. Or use in burritos or tacos. Or just keep the chili around to supplement vegetarian meals.

Prep time: 5 minutes
Cooking time: 5 hours
Makes 8 cups

RISOTTO AL SALTO

The Lazy Gourmet understands that sometimes nothing is lazier than eating leftovers. Of all my tricks for leftovers (chili burritos, leftover vegetable omelets), this is my best gourmet trick. Leftover risotto becomes a gorgeous golden cake, perfect with soup on a cold winter night.

1 cup leftover risotto
1 egg, beaten
1 tablespoon extra virgin olive oil or butter, divided
1 tablespoon grated Parmesan cheese

1. Combine the leftover risotto and the beaten egg.
2. Heat half the oil or butter in a 6-7-inch non-stick pan. Add risotto and spread it out so that it reaches the edges of the pan (more or less) so it resembles a flat pancake. Cook until browned on bottom. To check, wait 8 minutes or so and lift up the edge of the risotto with a spatula.
3. Place a flat plate over the pan and flip both over so the uncooked side is on bottom.
4. Add a little more oil or butter to the pan and slide the pancake in, browned side up. Cook until underside is browned.
5. Sprinkle with Parmesan and slice into serving pieces.

Total time: 20 minutes
Serves 2 as a side dish

FARRO AND
ROASTED BUTTERNUT SQUASH

My son-in-law Jonathan gets most of the credit for this recipe. We invented it together, but he makes it all the time to rave reviews. There are a couple of steps but each one is lazy by itself. And to be honest, this is really two simple recipes put together: Farro Pilaf and Roasted Butternut Squash. But together it is much more than the sum of its parts.

1/3 cup extra virgin olive oil
1 medium onion, diced
2 cups farro
2 cups chicken or vegetable stock
1 teaspoon salt
1 1 1/2-pound butternut squash, peeled and cut into 1/2-inch dice
2 tablespoon extra virgin olive oil
2 tablespoons maple syrup
1 teaspoon salt
Freshly ground black pepper
2 tablespoons minced sage or parsley leaves (or a combination of both)

1. Preheat oven to 400 degrees.
2. To make farro, heat oil in large saucepan. Add the onion and farro and sauté over medium heat for 20 minutes. Add stock and salt and bring to a boil. Cover, turn down heat, and cook for about 35 minutes until stock is absorbed.
3. To make squash (which you can peel and cut while the farro is cooking), in a large bowl, toss squash with oil, maple syrup, salt and pepper. Pour onto a large rimmed cookie sheet and bake 30 minutes, tossing halfway through.
4. In a large bowl, combine the cooked farro and the roasted squash. Toss with herbs.

Prep time: 35 minutes. Cooking time: 45 minutes, divided. Serves 6.

QUINOA PILAF

What makes a protein a protein? Amino acids. 8 essential ones, to be exact. Quinoa is a small beady-looking grain that plumps up like couscous. In ancient Incan civilization, it was one of three staple foods along with corn and potatoes. Quinoa contains all 8 essential amino acids, has a protein balance similar to that of milk, and is the only grain that is considered a complete protein. This means you don't need to serve it with beans or cheese or tofu or anything else to flush out its nutritional value. It's the perfect vegetarian side because it encompasses perfect vegetarian health (protein-wise, at least).

1 tablespoon extra virgin olive oil
1 medium onion, chopped
3 cloves garlic, peeled and minced or pressed
1 teaspoon ground cumin
1 teaspoon ground coriander
1 cup quinoa, rinsed
1 15-ounce can vegetarian stock (1 2/3 cup) or water
1/4 teaspoon salt
10 turns freshly ground black pepper
3/4 cup toasted almonds or pine nuts (optional)

1. Heat oil in a large saucepan. Sauté onion and garlic in oil until softened, about 3 minutes. Add cumin and coriander. Add quinoa.
2. Add stock. Bring to a boil, cover the pan, turn heat to low, and cook 15 minutes, until most of the quinoa grains have unfurled their small white tails. Uncover pan and cook 5 more minutes to evaporate excess liquid.
3. Stir in optional nuts.

Prep time: 10 minutes
Cooking time: 20 minutes
Serves 4

QUINOA PILAF WITH GARBANZO BEANS

Here is a not-so-carefully-guarded quinoa secret: around Passover, when diligent Ashkenazi Jews abstain from leavened carbohydrates, quinoa is permitted. The kosher rabbis who sit on the main kosher review boards in New York and Chicago have given quinoa the all-clear. So when springtime rolls around and your Kosher friends come to your house for dinner, play it safe and whip up this tasty (but elegant) potluck dish.

1 tablespoon extra virgin olive oil
1 onion, chopped
3 cloves garlic, peeled and minced
2 zucchini, chopped (or 2 red peppers, seeded and chopped)
2 teaspoons ground cumin
2 teaspoons ground coriander
1 cup quinoa, rinsed
1 15-ounce can vegetarian stock (1 2/3 cups)
1 14-ounce can garbanzo beans (2 cups), rinsed
3/4 cup loosely packed chopped cilantro (leaves and thin stems)
3 tablespoons pine nuts, toasted
Salt and freshly ground black pepper, to taste

1. Heat oil in a large sauce pan and sauté onion and garlic 3 minutes. Add zucchini or peppers and cumin and coriander and sauté 5 minutes. Add quinoa. Add stock and bring to a boil. Cover pan, turn heat to low, and cook 10 minutes. Add garbanzo beans and cook 10 minutes more.
2. Turn off heat, and toss quinoa with cilantro and pine nuts. Adjust seasoning.
3. Serve hot, warm, or cold.

Prep time: 15 minutes
Cooking time: 20 minutes
Serves 4

ZUCCHINI COUSCOUS

Couscous, a coarsely ground semolina pasta, is so lazy I'm almost embarrassed to write it into an official recipe. Here's a crash course in how to cook it: Pour couscous into bowl. Pour hot water over it. Let sit 5 minutes. Fluff with fork. Everything after that is frill. You can cook couscous using stock. You can flavor it with a variety of ground spices, dried fruit, or sautéed vegetables. Ask my cooking-contest-entering daughter and she would tell you about some amazing recipe made with couscous and fruit juice, or Jell-O (some of Josie's recipes are truly bizarre). But the bottom line is this: couscous is lazy. Serve this lazy, delicious side dish with roasted meat or rotisserie chicken and you're ready to dine.

1 1/2 pounds zucchini, washed and ends trimmed
1 tablespoon extra virgin olive oil
1 teaspoon ground cumin
1 1/2 teaspoons salt
7 turns freshly ground black pepper
1 cup water
2/3 cup couscous

1. Cut the zucchini into ¼-inch dice by cutting each zucchini into ¼-inch slices lengthwise, then cutting each slice into ¼-inch strips lengthwise, and then cutting crosswise into dice. This can be done in advance and the chopped zucchini stored in a plastic bag for a day or so.
2. Heat oil in a large sauté pan, and toss in zucchini, cumin, and salt and pepper. Cook over medium high heat until the zucchini is slightly browned. Add water and bring to a boil. Add couscous, turn off heat, cover pan, and wait 5 minutes.
3. The couscous can sit until the rest of the meal is done. Fluff before serving.

Prep time: 7 minutes
Cooking time: 15 minutes
Serves 4

Fish and Seafood

SALMON OR TUNA PICCATA
MUSTARD MINT SALMON
SWORDFISH, HALIBUT, OR TUNA WITH MANGO SALSA
RED-WINE OVEN-GLAZED SALMON
PAN-GLAZED SWORDFISH
HALIBUT WITH OLIVE TAPENADE AND PINE NUT CRUST
SEARED TUNA PEPPER STEAKS
TUNA, LANGUEDOC STYLE
CILANTRO AND SOY-MARINATED SEA BASS
SWORDFISH, HALIBUT, OR SEA BASS WITH GINGER
MARINADE
SOLE WITH LEMON AND CAPERS
SPEEDY SPICY PRAWNS
CRUSTY SCALLOPS

There are not enough good lazy fish recipes. That is, until now. And while I am sometimes guilty of fishing for compliments, I am never guilty of passing by the fish counter at the market. Just find a nice filet, and all you have to do is cook it for a few minutes, add a delicious topping, and sit down to eat. It doesn't get much lazier than that.

Modern times have made fish buying complicated, however. According to the Environmental Defense Fund, many fish populations are overfished and many farmed fish practices are harmful to the environment. I use the Seafood Watch pamphlet available from *www.seafoodwatch.org*; it lists the best fish choices, good alternatives, and seafood to avoid. All the recipes in this chapter use fish available farmed or wild that are also environmentally respectful.

SALMON OR TUNA PICCATA

In 41 years of marriage, Mark hasn't asked for much. On vacation, all he requires is the occasional dollop of Bruce Springsteen in the CD player and deep-dish pizza when we visit Chicago. Mark, though, is a Hawaii fiend, and when we go there our new MO is to rent a condo and cook for ourselves. This helps us avoid the tourist traps and gives us access to some of the best fish around—fresh from the local seaside fish market. When we last went to Maui, I bought some tuna and gussied it up with this simple lemon-caper cloak. I know, it's not very Hawaiian— but not everything from the tropics must be doused in pineapple. This recipe also works very nicely with fresh salmon.

Vegetable oil or oil spray
2 lemons
4 tuna or salmon filets
Salt and pepper
2 tablespoons capers
2 tablespoons butter, cut in 8 pieces
2 tablespoons parsley, minced (optional)

1. Preheat oven to 425 degrees.
2. Select a baking pan just large enough to hold all the fish. Oil the pan with oil or oil spray. Slice one lemon thinly and place the slices on the bottom of the pan. Place the fish on top of the lemon slices. Squeeze the other lemon over the salmon. Sprinkle the fish with salt, pepper, and capers and dot with the butter. Let rest 15 minutes.
3. Place baking pan on the middle shelf of pre-heated oven for about 15 minutes. If it looks like the juice is evaporating (lots of popping and hopping liquid) just add a tablespoon or two of water.
4. When the fish is cooked through, remove to serving dish, spoon sauce and fallen capers onto the fish, and sprinkle with parsley.

Prep time: 10 minutes. Cooking time: 20 minutes. Serves 4.

MUSTARD-MINT SALMON

This is another mystery-origin recipe. It came to me from my slightly less lazy but completely gourmet friends Janet and Peter. They did not invent it, however, so if you find it in a cookbook somewhere, shoot me a line and let me know the source. You will need a blender, but otherwise this recipe is blessed with a completely simple preparation. Combine ingredients and whiz electronically until smooth.

2 cloves garlic, peeled
1 1/2 tablespoons Dijon mustard
1 1/2 tablespoons coarse-grain mustard
3 tablespoons white wine vinegar
1/4 cup fresh mint leaves, packed
3/4 cup extra-virgin olive oil
Salt and pepper
1 1/2 pounds salmon or other firm fish, cut into 4 filets

1. Turn the blender on and, with it running, drop in garlic through the pouring spout to chop. Turn off blender and add mustards, vinegar, and mint. Turn blender on again. With the machine running, pour in olive oil slowly. It will emulsify, like a thin mayonnaise. Add salt and pepper to taste. You can make this 3-4 days in advance and refrigerate until using.
2. Preheat oven to 425 degrees. Place the fish in a baking pan that has been sprayed or rubbed with oil. Sprinkle with salt and pepper and bake for 15 minutes. Test for doneness.
3. Serve fish with sauce on the side.

Prep time: 10 minutes
Cooking time: 15–20 minutes
Serves 4

SWORDFISH, HALIBUT, OR TUNA WITH MANGO SALSA

I love retirement. It allows me to read the morning paper cover to cover, write a cookbook, and take watercolor classes at the Hui No'eau Visual Arts Center in Makawao, Maui. Now, if you're living an artist's life in Hawaii, do you really want to spend your time trapped in the kitchen? You do not. Triple the recipe and serve it three nights in a row. Pure bliss.

1 large ripe mango
2 red onions
1 red or yellow bell pepper
1 serrano chile
2 cloves garlic
1/3 bunch cilantro
1 lime
Salt and freshly ground pepper, to taste
2 avocados (optional)
1 1/2 pounds halibut or tuna, cut into 4 portions

1. Peel, seed and cut the mango into ¾-inch pieces. Finely dice the red onions. Seed the red or yellow bell pepper and cut into ¾-inch dice. Finely mince the chile and garlic. Mince the cilantro. Place all ingredients in a large bowl. Squeeze lime over the mixture. Add salt and pepper to taste. If using avocados, remove skin and pit, cut flesh into ¾-inch pieces, and add to the bowl. Toss gently.
2. Preheat oven to 425 degrees. Place the fish in a baking pan that has been sprayed or rubbed with oil. Sprinkle with salt and pepper and bake for 15 minutes. Test for doneness.
3. Serve the salsa on top of the fish.

Prep time: 15 minutes. Cooking time: 15–20 minutes. Makes 3 cups. Serves 4.

RED-WINE OVEN-GLAZED SALMON

Nothing is easier than a glaze and nothing makes you feel like a culinary artist like cooking with a paintbrush. This is pretty much a dump in pot, stir, and simmer dish.

1-inch piece peeled ginger, grated (not minced)
1/2 cup soy sauce
1 cup red wine
1/2 cup mirin or cooking sherry
2 tablespoons packed dark brown sugar
1 teaspoon lime juice
4 salmon steaks or filets

1. Make glaze: Combine first five ingredients in a small saucepan, bring to a boil, and cook over medium-low heat until syrupy, around 10 minutes. Cool. Add lime juice. The glaze can be made ahead of time and stored in fridge.
2. Preheat oven to 400 degrees. Line a cookie sheet with parchment paper and paint or spray with cooking oil (the sauce is sugary and will burn onto the pan if you don't). About 5 minutes before cooking, paint salmon with the glaze. Silicon cooking brushes are easy to clean and surprisingly useful.
3. Bake 15 minutes (watch for burning). Test for doneness.
4. Serve with extra glaze on the side.

Note: This recipe makes enough glaze for 8-10 filets, so you can save the extra glaze for another meal.

Prep time: 15 minutes
Cooking time: 15 minutes
Serves 4

PAN-GLAZED SWORDFISH

I like to cook the fish all at the same time so that it will come to the table at once, hot and ready to eat. But because I don't have one sauté pan that's big enough, I use two pans when I make this dish. I have a dishwasher. His name is Mark and and when God made Mark, God broke the mold (although the dishes stayed in one piece). If you do not have a Mark, you do not have to use two pans for this recipe. You can cook in batches and use one.

1/4 cup sugar
25 turns freshly ground black pepper
2 pounds swordfish steaks (4 steaks)
1-2 tablespoons peanut oil
1/4 cup soy sauce
1 tablespoon sesame seeds

1. Combine sugar and pepper on a plate. Over a medium high flame, heat a large sauté pan or two smaller ones, large enough to hold all the swordfish in one layer,
2. When the pans are hot, add oil to each pan. Dip one side of swordfish in sugar mixture and place sugar side down in saucepan over medium high heat. Cook over medium high heat until browned, about 4-5 minutes.
3. Turn down the heat to medium low, add the soy sauce, cover the pan, and cook until the swordfish is just opaque, about 4-5 more minutes. The soy sauce will bubble furiously until the heat goes down.
4. Place fish on plates or serving platter, glazed side up. Pour sauce over the fish and sprinkle with sesame seeds.

Total time: 15 minutes
Serves 4-6

HALIBUT WITH OLIVE TAPENADE AND PINE NUT CRUST

Yes, tapenade (olive paste) is available in jars from the grocery store, but have you seen the price tag for a 3-ounce portion? It's ridiculous when you can so easily make your own olive paste at home with a few easy-to-keep-on-hand ingredients. All you need are olives (imperishable), capers (imperishable), oil (imperishable), garlic (semi-perishable), and anchovy paste (virtually imperishable). And you should definitely always have pine nuts around. I buy big bags at Costco and keep them in the freezer. They are nice toasted and sprinkled on salads, in pasta, ground into pesto, or used to make a nice crust for fish, as in this recipe.

1/2 cup tapenade or olive paste (see recipe on page 106)
1/2 cup pine nuts
1 cup seasoned croutons
4 halibut filets
Salt and freshly ground black pepper

1. Preheat oven to 425 degrees.
2. Toast pine nuts carefully in a toaster oven or in a small sauté pan on the stove until they are light brown. They burn easily, so keep an eye on them. Cool 5 minutes. Place pine nuts in a food processor and pulse a few times. Add croutons and process until crumbly.
3. Grease a baking pan with oil or oil spray and place halibut in pan. Press 2 tablespoons of olive paste or tapenade on top of each filet. Cover olive paste with crouton-pine nut mixture, divided evenly among the filets.
4. Bake 15 minutes.

Prep time: 10 minutes
Cooking time: 15 minutes
Serves 4

OLIVE TAPENADE

This is a little simpler than a classic tapenade. But this is the lazy gourmet's lazy version. If you want to make classic tapenade, it's pretty easy: you can find a recipe on the Internet.

1 cup Kalamata olives, pitted
1/4 cup basil leaves, julienned
1 anchovy filet, rinsed, or 1/2 inch anchovy paste
2 tablespoons extra virgin olive oil
15 turns freshly ground black pepper

Place all ingredients in a food processor, and pulse until a chunky sauce forms.

How to use olive tapenade:
1. Serve it on fish or chicken.
2. Mix a tablespoon of tapenade with a teaspoon of vinegar and a tablespoon of olive oil to make a tapenade vinaigrette for fish or chicken.

Prep time: 5 minutes
Makes around 1 cup

SEARED TUNA PEPPER STEAKS

Sherry wine makes some think of little old ladies. It makes me think of Asian food. Instead of nipping from the sherry bottle in your golden years, use it as a substitute for mirin. It makes a great addition to Asian-flavored marinades and is the perfect deglazing liquid for a no-fuss sauce like the kind detailed in this quick and easy recipe.

4 tuna steaks
1 tablespoon cracked black peppercorns
1 tablespoon vegetable oil
2 teaspoons sesame oil
1/4 cup dry sherry or mirin
1/4 cup soy sauce
1 tablespoon sesame seeds

1. Press black pepper into tuna steaks.
2. Heat large sauté pan over medium heat. Add vegetable oil and sesame oil. Place tuna steaks in a pan and cook until done, about 3 minutes per side or longer if you want it less rare.
3. Remove steaks. To cooking pan, add sherry or mirin and soy sauce and boil down a little. Spoon over steaks and sprinkle with sesame seeds.

Total time: 15 minutes
Serves 4

TUNA, LANGUEDOC STYLE

I think I "borrowed" this recipe from the late great magazine *Gourmet*. The problem with my recipe files is that they tend to start from someone else's inspiration and morph wildly from there. Josie tells me that I need to be more cognizant of ownership—she's a cooking contest maven and is always Googling her own creations to make sure they are, in fact, original. But I think the best cooking comes from being inspired by what's around you, what you see and eat, and yes, what you cook. The cleanup is fast and the cooking is even faster.

4 tuna steaks
Salt and freshly ground black pepper
2 tablespoons extra virgin olive oil
12 cloves garlic, peeled and sliced
Thyme from 8 sprigs
Juice of two lemons

1. Salt and pepper the tuna steaks.
2. Heat large skillet. When hot, add olive oil and sauté steaks until cooked to your liking. If you like them cooked through, 4 minutes per side is usually good. (Remember that tuna dries out if cooked too long and it keeps cooking even after you take if off the heat.) Remove the tuna to plate and keep warm.
3. Reduce heat, add garlic and thyme, and sauté until the garlic is lightly golden. Add lemon juice and cook to reduce slightly. Pour over steaks.

Time: 10 minutes
Serves 4

CILANTRO AND SOY-MARINATED SEA BASS

Despite the skills of my dishwashing husband, the sign of a good lazy recipe can sometimes be its lack of dirty dishes. Marinating is so easy in part because you can marinate almost anything in a gallon plastic bag. When the marinating part is done, rinse out the bag, dry it, and label it "fish" with a Sharpie. Then keep it in the freezer until next time you marinate fish.

4 cloves garlic
1 jalapeno, stemmed and seeded, or 1/4 teaspoon red pepper flakes
1 cup cilantro, including leaves and smaller stems
1/2 cup soy sauce
10 turns pepper
4 seabass filets

1. In a food processor or blender, mince the garlic and jalapeño (if using) by dropping it through the opening in the top of the blender. Add the cilantro and process until minced. Add the soy sauce and process.
2. Put fish in a 1-gallon plastic bag and add marinade. Marinate 15 minutes.
3. Grill, broil, or bake fish to your liking, around 7 minutes per side.

Prep time: 15 minutes
Marinating time: 15 minutes–2 hours
Cooking time: 14 minutes
Serves 4

SWORDFISH, HALIBUT, OR SEA BASS WITH GINGER MARINADE

When it comes to Asian flavors, nothing skews an otherwise normal meal towards the Far East than a dollop of ginger. The "best" way to prepare ginger is to grate it, which releases the most juice and therefore flavor. A company called The Ginger People produces a wonderful grated ginger paste sold in a jar that you can substitute for fresh ginger. Classic lazy gourmets should just keep ginger root in the house.

1 tablespoon grated ginger (about a 1-inch piece, before grating)
1 small clove garlic, pressed with a garlic press
2 tablespoons sesame oil
3 tablespoons soy sauce
1 tablespoon mirin or dry sherry
Juice of one lemon
2 pounds halibut, swordfish, or sea bass

1. Combine first 6 ingredients in a small bowl.
2. Place fish in a 1-gallon zip lock bag.
3. Pour marinade over the fish in the bag and refrigerate until ready to use, but not more than 8 hours.
4. Remove fish from bag (discard marinade) and grill or broil to your liking, 7 minutes a side.

Prep time: 10 minutes
Marinating time: 15 minutes–8 hours
Cooking time: 15 minutes
Serves 4–5

SOLE WITH LEMON AND CAPERS

When my girls were 7 and 5, Mark and I plucked them out of school and brought them to France for a couple of months. We went to white-sand beaches, took them through museums, and all the way up the Eiffel Tower. Now, 25 years later, all they can remember is that they found a bird dying on the ground in a park, and that for dinner one night we ate sole that was from a moat outside the medieval-style castle we stayed in. That both incidents involve animals dying worries me. But this recipe is still a nice memento.

1/4 cup flour
1 teaspoon salt
1 teaspoon paprika
Ground pepper to taste
1 1/2 pounds sole filets
6 tablespoons butter, divided
1 tablespoon vegetable oil
1/2 cup dry white wine
1 tablespoon capers, rinsed
Juice of one lemon
Chopped parsley, for garnish (optional)

1. Combine flour with salt, pepper and paprika on a medium sized dish. Coat sole in flour. Heat 2 tablespoons of butter and the oil in a wide saucepan and sauté the sole 2 to 3 minutes on a side, until slightly golden. (You may have to do this in batches so you don't crowd the pan.) Remove fish to a serving plate and keep warm.
2. Discard any extra oil in the pan. Over medium heat, melt the remaining 4 tablespoons of butter. Add the capers. After a minute, add the wine and boil 2 or 3 minutes, scraping up any bits left in the pan. Add the lemon juice and cook until slightly thickened, another minute. Pour over the fish and sprinkle with parsley.

Prep time: 5 minutes. Cooking time: 15 minutes. Serves 4.

SPEEDY SPICY PRAWNS

There is nothing wrong with buying frozen shrimp. Most fish markets sell shrimp that has been frozen and defrosted anyway, so why not skip a step? In fact, why not skip two steps and buy peeled frozen shrimp? With pre-peeled, frozen crustaceans on hand you can defrost these little guys as needed by putting a handful in a bowl and running cold water over them. Then you've got gourmet dining anytime.

1/2 cup hoisin sauce
1/2 cup orange juice
1 teaspoon Chinese chili paste with garlc, or more to taste
1/4 bunch cilantro, chopped (2 tablespoons reserved)
1 bunch green onions, chopped (2 tablespoons reserved)
1/4 cup extra virgin olive oil
2 pounds large raw prawns (21-25 to a pound), peeled and deveined

1. In a bowl, mix together hoisin sauce, orange juice, chili paste, cilantro, green onions, and olive oil. Put prawns in 1-gallon zip lock bag and add sauce. Shake bag to coat shrimp in marinade and let marinate 15 minutes at room temperature, or refrigerate for at least 1 hour and up to 3 hours.
2. Preheat oven to 375 degrees. Remove shrimp from marinade with a slotted spoon and place on a baking sheet with a rim. Discard marinade. Bake for 11 minutes or until shrimp has turned pink all over.
3. Transfer to a serving platter and garnish with reserved cilantro and green onion.

Prep time: 10 minutes
Marinating time: 15 minutes–3 hours
Cooking time: 11 minutes
Serves 4 for a main course
Serves 8 as an hors d'oeuvre

CRUSTY SCALLOPS

Cousin Alice is not fond of cooking, and therefore does not spend excessive amounts of time in the kitchen. Yet she has prepared more than her fair share of dinner parties for foreign visitors, as well as for me and my family. Her recipes are easy and elegant enough for any type of entertaining. This scallop recipe is a prime example of Alice's gourmet style. If cooking for more than four, double or triple the recipe as needed.

1 1/2 pounds large scallops
3 tablespoons butter
Salt and freshly ground black pepper
2 tablespoons all-purpose flour (divided)
1/2 teaspoon paprika (divided)

1. Preheat broiler.
2. Place the scallops in a broiler-safe pan or casserole dish just large enough to hold them in a single layer. Melt the butter and pour it over the scallops in the pan and toss, adding salt and pepper. Sprinkle the top with 1 tablespoon flour and ¼ teaspoon paprika.
3. Place scallops under broiler for 5 minutes. Turn the scallops over so the other side browns (you can do this quickly, it doesn't have to be perfect) and sprinkle with rest of flour and paprika. Broil another 4 minutes until done.

Total time: 15 minutes
Serves 4

Chicken and Poultry

My father's parents were from Hungary and I like to think I would have done well there. I imagine myself in a shtetl, raising chickens. I love poultry and cook it far too frequently to win any humanitarian awards from my youngest daughter. Of course, had I lived way back when in Hungary, none of these recipes would have been lazy (killing, poaching, plucking and all that). Now, thanks to modern butchery, boned, skinned, and de-gizzarded chicken is a staple in any self-respecting lazy cook's kitchen.

To be sure chicken is cooked through,

• Use a meat thermometer. Cook boneless chicken to 160°F; cook chicken on the bone to 170°F.

• Juices should run clear, not pink, when chicken is pierced with a fork. (When in doubt, remove the chicken to a plate and cut it with a knife to be sure the meat is opaque and no longer pink in the center.)

TARRAGON GARLIC CHICKEN

This is the perfect recipe for the truly lazy gourmet, and by that I mean it's the perfect recipe for my daughter's friend Katie. Katie cooks mostly when the ingredients can be poured (or scooped) into a bowl and eaten with a spoon. Although this recipe doesn't come in a bowl, and you might need a fork and knife to eat it, it's lazy to the extreme and dedicated to her.

2 pounds of chicken on the bone, dark and/or light meat
2 tablespoons vegetable oil
10 turns freshly ground black pepper
2 teaspoons garlic salt
2 teaspoons dried tarragon or rosemary (not both)

1. Preheat broiler. Line broiler pan with foil (to facilitate easy cleanup).
2. Rub chicken with oil, and sprinkle with pepper, garlic salt, and either tarragon or rosemary. Place chicken on broiler pan. Broil about 4 inches from broiler, 20-25 minutes, turning once, about halfway through. You may have to broil the dark meat for an extra few minutes.

Prep time: 10 minutes
Cooking time: 20-25 minutes
Serves 4

CHICKEN WITH SAGE AND WINE

This recipe was the main staple in my kitchen for at least two decades. It takes practically no work and the wine sauce is scrumptious.

4 chicken breasts on the bone, skin on
Salt and freshly ground black pepper
4 tablespoons butter, divided
1 tablespoon extra virgin olive oil
1 tablespoon fresh sage leaves
Several cloves garlic, peeled
3/4 cup dry white wine or combination of white wine and chicken
    stock

1. Sprinkle the chicken on all sides with salt and pepper. Heat 2 tablespoons butter and the olive oil in a large saucepan. When foam from the butter subsides, brown chicken on both sides over medium high heat, about 5 minutes a side.
2. Add sage leaves, garlic, and wine to the pan. Cover, lower the heat to medium and cook 20 minutes, or until the chicken is cooked through.
3. Remove chicken and keep warm. Adjust heat to medium-high and boil wine until syrupy. Remove pan from heat and stir in remaining butter.
4. Serve chicken with sauce, and rice, noodles, or bread to soak up the sauce.

Prep time: 5 minutes
Cooking time: 30 minutes
Serves 4

YOGURT MUSTARD CHICKEN

This recipe comes from Lydie Marshall's book *Chez Nous: Home Cooking from the South of France*. My daughter adores this recipe and calls to ask for the proper mustard-to-yogurt ratio every month. I suppose she knows she could just write it down, but it's a nice little ritual and so when she gets her copy of *The Lazy Gourmet*, I may just have to deliver it missing a page.

1 1/2 cups plain nonfat yogurt
1/3 cup Dijon mustard
1 tablespoon fresh thyme leaves, or 2 teaspoons dried thyme
Pinch of salt
Freshly ground black pepper
4 skinless chicken breast halves, bone in

1. Preheat oven to 400 degrees.
2. Mix together all ingredients except the chicken in a 9 x 13-inch baking pan. Dredge the chicken in the yogurt mixture until well coated. Arrange chicken pieces in the pan so that there is space between them. This will allow the sauce to cook down. Put pan in the oven immediately. (Chicken can also marinate in yogurt mixture overnight in the refrigerator.)
3. Bake chicken 40 minutes until golden.
4. Transfer chicken to serving plate. Pour the curdled yogurt sauce into a blender or food processor and blend. A smooth sauce will form. Serve with rice or noodles to soak up the delicious sauce.

Alternatives: You can make this with boneless skinless chicken breasts; in that case, make the marinade with 1 cup yogurt and ¼ cup mustard. Bake 20 minutes and run under the broiler to add some color (the chicken will be whiter in color than on the chicken on the bone, but the sauce will be the same).

Prep time: 5 minutes. Cooking time: 40 minutes. Serves 4.

CHICKEN NIÇOISE

Ah, France. I traveled there for the first time in the summer after my junior year in high school. That trip marked my first plane trip and the first time I'd been away from home. I loved every minute of it. The family I lived with had a wood-burning stove in the kitchen and I spent a lot of time there with the maid, Marie-Louise, who was in charge of all the cooking. Despite the presence of a maid and the fact that my host family was comfortably well off, this was in 1963 and the country had not yet fully recovered from World War II. As a 17-year-old, I didn't have much awareness of the situation, but what I do remember is my first French meal. Bread was put on the table, and we all broke off pieces of it. There was a cheese course, and a salad course, both of which would be a lovely addition to this next recipe.

2 tablespoons extra virgin olive oil, divided
4 boneless chicken breast halves
Salt and freshly ground black pepper
1 clove garlic, peeled
2 Roma tomatoes, cut in quarters, or 1 1/2 cups cherry tomatoes
8 kalamata olives, pitted
1 tablespoon capers, drained
1 tablespoon sherry vinegar

1. Heat 1 tablespoon oil in a heavy-bottomed nonstick sauté pan. Sprinkle the chicken evenly with salt and pepper. When the oil is shimmering, sauté the chicken over medium-high heat for 6-8 minutes per side or until cooked through.
2. While chicken cooks, put peeled garlic in food processor and chop. Add tomatoes, olives, capers, and salt and pepper to taste. Process until chunky. Turn tomato sauce out into a bowl and add remaining 1 tablespoon oil and the vinegar.
3. Serve chicken with a dollop of the sauce.

Prep time: 10 minutes. Cooking time: around 15 minutes. Serves 4.

CHICKEN WITH CIDER VINEGAR AND MUSTARD MARINADE

White meat is low in fat and cholesterol and so, with an eye to my and Mark's health, we eat a lot of it. The one downside to the chicken breast is that without streaks of nice rich fat to keep it moist, it dries out easily. Enter my friend The Marinade. Marinating chicken is a good anti-dehydration measure and usually means your chicken can be prepped in advance—the ultimate lazy dream.

1/4 cup brown sugar
3 cloves garlic, peeled and minced or pressed
1/4 cup cider vinegar
Juice of one lemon or lime
3 tablespoons grainy mustard
1/4 cup extra virgin olive oil
10 turns freshly ground black pepper
1 teaspoon salt
4 boneless skinless chicken breast halves

1. In a small bowl, combine all ingredients except the chicken. Place the chicken in a 1-gallon zip lock bag. Pour in the marinade and seal the bag. Refrigerate 1 to 24 hours.
2. When you're ready to cook, preheat the oven to 350 degrees. Place the chicken and marinade in a baking dish. Bake 20-30 minutes depending on the size of the chicken pieces. Test for doneness.
3. Serve with marinade.

Prep time: 10 minutes
Marinating time: 1-24 hours
Cooking time: 30 minutes
Serves 4

QUICK AND EASY GRILLED CHICKEN WITH SALAD DRESSING

Those of you who like your recipes neatly laid out with exact direction won't like this one, but if you don't try it you'll be missing out. Exact measurements are fine and dandy most of the time, but for something this easy and impossible to mess up, sling your shoulders back, use your creativity, and you'll find that this is the best recipe concept to hit your lazy kitchen in years. We use boned chicken breasts for parties, especially for summer BBQs and kid-friendly occasions. After cooking, the chicken can be cut in slices for sandwiches or chicken salad.

1 3-4 pound chicken, in pieces (bone-in or boneless), white or
    dark meat
Your favorite bottled salad dressing

1. Put the chicken pieces in a zip lock bag. Pour salad dressing over them. Marinate in the refrigerator, at least 15 minutes or as long as overnight in the refrigerator.
2. Remove the chicken from the marinade, shaking off excess. Grill, pan fry, or bake chicken at 350 degrees until done. Chicken on the bone cooks for about 40 minutes in the oven. Boneless breasts cook 7 minutes a side on the grill. If you use a grill, don't forget to clean the grill top, using tongs to rub it with a paper towel dipped in oil, so the chicken won't stick.

Prep time: 2 minutes
Marinating time: 15 minutes–24 hours
Cooking Time: 20–40 minutes
Serves 4

CHICKEN WITH CILANTRO SOY MARINADE

Rules for marinating chicken the night before: Put on your PJs and slippers, head to the kitchen, and place chicken in a zip lock bag. Add marinate ingredients to the bag, seal, and pop it in the refrigerator. Now go to sleep. Of course, you can also just put the marinade and the chicken directly in the baking dish you plan to use, but if your refrigerator is as full as mine is (with nothing but lazy ingredients), you won't have room to do that!

4 cloves garlic, peeled
1 cup roughly chopped cilantro leaves and stems
1/2 teaspoon red pepper flakes
1/4 cup plus 2 tablespoons soy sauce
4 boneless skinless chicken breast halves

1. Drop the garlic into a blender and mince. Add cilantro and mince. Add pepper and soy sauce and combine.
2. Put chicken in a 1-gallon zip lock bag. Pour marinade over chicken. Refrigerate at least 1 hour and up to 24 hours.
3. Bake 20-30 minutes at 350 degrees or grill on medium heat for 7 minutes per side.

Prep time: 5 minutes
Marinating time: 1-24 hours
Cooking time: 15-30 minutes
Serves 4

LEMON GARLIC CHICKEN

This is dish is stellar enough for company, especially when you want to impress important guests like visiting parents. (Hint, hint, kids.)

7 cloves garlic, peeled
20 turns freshly ground black pepper
Zest from 2 lemons
1/2 teaspoon dried thyme
1/2 cup dry white wine
Juice from 2 lemons
1/4 cup olive oil
4 boneless skinless chicken breast halves

1. In a food processor or blender, chop up the garlic
2. Add pepper, lemon zest, thyme, wine, lemon juice and olive oil. Blend or pulse and watch your marinade form.
3. Place chicken in a 1-gallon zip lock bag. Pour marinade over chicken and refrigerate at least 1 hour and up to 24 hours.
4. Preheat oven to 350 degrees. Put chicken and marinade in baking pan. Bake 25 minutes. Before serving, strain the marinade into a fat separator and pour out the fat. Serve the rest as a sauce. If you grill or broil the chicken, put the marinade in a saucepan, bring to a boil, and simmer for a few minutes. Strain into a fat separator, pour out the fat, and serve as a sauce.

Prep time: 15 minutes
Marinating time: 1-24 hours
Baking time: 25 minutes
Serves 4

LAZY CHICKEN CURRY

There are a lot of ingredients in this recipe but don't let that intimidate you. Except for the chicken and cilantro, all can be kept in your house forever, or in the case of ginger and onion, almost forever.

1-inch piece ginger, peeled
1 medium onion, roughly chopped
2 teaspoons ground cumin
2 teaspoons ground coriander
1/2 teaspoon turmeric
1/2 teaspoon cinnamon
1/4 teaspoon cayenne pepper
1 1/2 teaspoons salt
15 turns freshly ground black pepper
2 tablespoons water
2 tablespoons canola oil
Juice of 1 lemon
1 14-ounce can chopped tomatoes, drained
1 1/2-2 pounds boneless skinless chicken breast halves, each cut in
    4 squarish pieces
2 tablespoons chopped cilantro

1. Mince the ginger in the food processor. Add the onion and pulse 4 or 5 times. Add cumin, coriander, turmeric, cinnamon, cayenne, salt and pepper, and water and process until medium-chunky.
2. In a medium saucepan, sauté onion mixture in oil over medium heat until water has almost all evaporated and onions start to brown around edges, 5-6 minutes. Add lemon juice and tomatoes to saucepan and cook 2 minutes. Add chicken, stir to coat, bring to simmer, cover and cook 10-15 minutes. Remove cover and boil away excess liquid. Sprinkle with cilantro and serve over rice.

Prep time: 15 minutes. Cooking time: 20 minutes. Serves 4.

CRUSHED HERB CHICKEN

Yes, I suppose you could buy a spice blend and make this chicken. But spice blends can get quite stale and lose their flavor. Your own spices are easier to keep track of, and this particular blend creates a nice ginger-herb flavor—very East meets West. You don't actually need the food processor here; simply chop up the garlic and mix it with salt and then add the other ingredients. Or if you want to get super fancy, mash up the garlic and spices with a mortar and pestle. But that sounds like work, doesn't it?

4 cloves garlic, peeled
1 1/2 teaspoons salt
20 turns freshly ground black pepper
2 teaspoons powdered ginger
4 bay leaves
2 teaspoons dried thyme
2 teaspoons dried sage
2 teaspoons dried marjoram (optional)
1/4 cup soy sauce
1/4 cup extra virgin olive oil
3 pounds chicken pieces on the bone

1. In a small food processor, mince the garlic and salt. Add all other ingredients except chicken and blend. Rub the marinade on the chicken and refrigerate overnight in a covered bowl or zip lock bag.
2. Preheat the oven to 350 degrees. Place marinated chicken in a baking dish. Bake for 45 minutes or until done. (Breasts cook a little faster and can be taken out of the oven after 30 minutes.)

Prep time: 10 minutes
Marinating time: 8 hours or more
Cooking time: 45 minutes
Serves 4

DRY BARBECUE RUB FOR CHICKEN

There's nothing like a barbecue supper. Just make sure to get a head count before you fire up the grill. At my daughter's pre-wedding barbecue, there must have been 65 people in attendance and we ran out of food 45 minutes into it. That wouldn't have happened if someone (not naming names, ahem, BRIDE) had kept better track of the RSVP list.

2 tablespoons brown sugar
1 tablespoon salt
20 turns freshly ground black pepper
2 tablespoons paprika
1 teaspoon garlic powder
1 teaspoon onion powder
1/4 teaspoon cayenne pepper
3 pounds chicken parts, bone in

1. Preheat the oven to 400 degrees.
2. In a small bowl, combine all the ingredients except the chicken. Rub the spice mixture on the chicken.
3. Arrange the chicken skin side up in an oiled baking dish. Bake for 30-40 minutes or until done. Cook the dark meat a little longer. This can also be broiled or grilled.

Prep time: 5 minutes
Cooking time: 30–45 minutes
Serves 4

CHICKEN WITH OLIVES, PRUNES, AND CAPERS

This recipe is inspired by the *Silver Palate Cookbook*, although I did make a few changes, starting with the name. They called it Chicken Marbella, which is just so old-sounding. This sweet and tart dish is perfect for a dinner party of 10-12 people. Or just you. And many leftovers.

25 cloves garlic, peeled and minced (preferably in small Cuisinart)
3/4 cup extra virgin olive oil
1 3/4 cups dry white wine
1/2 cup balsamic vinegar
1/2 cup red wine vinegar
2 tablespoons dried oregano leaves
5 bay leaves
1 cup plus 2 tablespoons pitted Kalamata olives
1 cup plus 2 tablespoons capers, drained and rinsed
2 1/4 cups pitted prunes
1 teaspoon salt and 1 teaspoon freshly ground black pepper
16 pieces of chicken, skin on (mixture of breasts, legs, and thighs)
4 1/2 tablespoons chopped cilantro

1. Combine all the ingredients except the chicken and cilantro. Put the chicken into 2 half-gallon freezer bags. Divide the marinade evenly between the two bags and refrigerate overnight.
2. Preheat oven to 350 degrees. Put the chicken and marinade in two baking dishes. Make sure the olives, capers, and prunes are evenly scattered about. Let the chicken come to room temperature. Bake for about an hour. Sprinkle with cilantro before serving.

Prep time: 30 minutes. Marinating time: 8 hours or more.
Cooking time: 1 hour. Serves 10-12.

TURKEY BALSAMICO

When I was in college, I spent a month in Italy studying Italian. An older woman ran the *pensione* where I stayed, and she taught me how to swear in Italian. Her son was a pilot, and he showed me around on his motor bike. You can see that this woman was a very useful connection to have. And that's without counting this recipe for Turkey Balsamico. I think the original version used veal, but veal is hard to find, expensive, and not very politically correct.

1 1/2 pounds skinless turkey breast, cut into 2-inch pieces
2 tablespoons butter
1 cup all-purpose flour
1/4 cup balsamic vinegar
Salt and freshly ground black pepper

1. Dry turkey with paper towels. Coat with the flour. Melt butter in a non-stick sauté pan. When the butter has foamed up and then the bubbles have subsided, add the turkey and cook it 3 minutes per side, adding salt and pepper while it cooks.
2. When the turkey is slightly browned all over, add balsamic vinegar and cook 6-8 minutes until cooked through. The meat will be coated with a syrupy balsamic glaze.

Prep time: 5 minutes
Cooking time: 15 minutes
Serves 4

TURKEY ALL'ARRABBIATA

Another Italian-inspired recipe. Note that everything except the turkey is imperishable, assuming you have sage in the garden. This is almost as easy as Turkey Balsamico but has a more complex flavor. And it's delicious.

1 tablespoon butter
1 tablespoon olive extra virgin oil
1 clove garlic, peeled
Sage leaves from 1 bunch sage
1/4 teaspoon pepper flakes
1 1/2 pounds skinless turkey breast, cut into 2-inch pieces
1 cup all-purpose flour
Salt and freshly ground black pepper
1 tablespoon balsamic vinegar
1/2 cup marsala wine
1 tablespoon tomato paste

1. In a large saucepan, heat the butter and olive oil to medium and sauté garlic, sage, and peperoncino until the garlic gives off an aroma.
2. Dry turkey with paper towels and toss with flour. Don't do this ahead of time or the meat will get soggy.
3. Add turkey to garlic and sage mixture and sauté to brown. Add salt and pepper to taste while it cooks.
4. When the turkey is browned slightly all over, add the balsamic vinegar and cook a few seconds to evaporate. Add marsala wine and tomato paste and cook 5 minutes or so until a thick sauce forms.

Prep time: 10 minutes
Cooking time: 15 minutes
Serves 4

Meat

BEEF
LAMB
PORK

Thanks to rising cholesterol counts, the dangers of clogged arteries, and the lasting legacy of vegetarian teenagers, Mark and I don't eat much meat at home anymore. Luckily for readers of this cookbook, there are some excellent exceptions. Flank steak is a lazy gourmet's bosom buddy: simply marinate and grill. Brisket lends itself easily to long, slow, no-fuss cooking. Lamb gussies up any dinner party. (And just a note: I love lamb, but there is a real difference in quality between the best lamb and the others. Only use the best.) Finally, I confess to a lasting affection for pork tenderloin—another easily marinate-able meat.

Beef

FLANK STEAK IN SESAME TERIYAKI MARINADE
BOEUF BOURGUIGNON
HANUKKAH BRISKET
BRISKET WITH PRUNES
STEAK WITH RED WINE BUTTER SAUCE

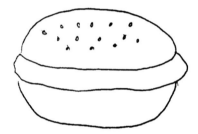

FLANK STEAK IN SESAME TERIYAKI MARINADE

My kids ate this every week of their childhood until they reached their teenage years and became vegetarians. For working parents, there's no meal that is lazier and more well-received—especially when served with tater tots.

You should note that all meat is completely freezer-friendly. Buy a nice amount, seal in a big freezer bag, and you can keep it on hand for those carnivorous cravings. Flank steak can even be marinated as it defrosts. Simply pour marinade into the bag the meat is frozen in, reseal, and marinate in the fridge until meat defrosts. How lazy is that?

1/2 cup mirin (Japanese sweet wine)
1/2 cup low-sodium soy sauce
2 tablespoons light brown sugar
2 cloves garlic, peeled and smashed
1 1/2-inch slice ginger, smashed
2 teaspoons sesame oil
2 pounds flank steak

1. Combine marinade ingredients (mirin, soy sauce, brown sugar, garlic, ginger, and sesame oil) in a small saucepan. Bring to a boil and simmer for 5 minutes. Let cool.
2. Place steak in a large plastic bag and add marinade. Marinate in the refrigerator at least 12 hours, or overnight.
3. Remove meat from marinade, and barbecue or broil 5 or 6 minutes a side, depending on size and degree of doneness you want. Let it rest 5 minutes. Slice the meat across the grain, and serve.

Prep time: 5 minutes
Marinating time: At least 12 hours
Cooking time: 15 minutes
Serves 4–6

BOEUF BOURGUIGNON

Two confessions up front: First, there are two non-lazy elements in the classic French version of this recipe. I've eliminated one, which is using pearl onions. Without them, the taste isn't affected at all, but I just thought you should know. The second non-lazy step is essential, which is browning the meat. It isn't hard, just not lazy. From that point on, classic French Boeuf Bourguignon is straightforward and unfussy. It's a perfect dish for company—just make it in advance so you're unencumbered on the day of the event. Then serve with warm baguette and a simple salad.

2 1/2 pounds stew beef, cut into 2-inch cubes
1/4 cup extra virgin olive oil
4 cloves garlic, peeled and minced
Salt and freshly ground black pepper
1 6-ounce can tomato paste
3 cups French Burgundy wine (Pinot Noir)
2 cups beef broth
3 bay leaves
6 sprigs thyme
3 6-inch sprigs of rosemary
1 pound small red potatoes, quartered
1/2 pound small carrots
2 small onions, quartered
1 pound mushrooms, quartered
4 stalks celery, cut into 2-inch pieces
2 tablespoons cornstarch (optional)
4 tablespoons parsley, minced

1. Dry meat using paper towels. In a 5-quart heavy casserole pot or Dutch oven, brown the meat in oil over medium-high heat. (Do this in batches—if you brown too many pieces at a time, they steam instead of browning.) Set the pieces of meat aside on a plate as soon as they are done. When all the meat is browned, return it to the pan, sprinkle with garlic and salt and pepper, and cook over medium heat for 5 minutes, tossing from time to time.

2. While meat cooks, combine tomato paste, wine, and broth in a medium bowl. Pour the liquid over the meat, add the bay leaves, thyme, and rosemary to the pot. Bring the stew to a boil, cover, turn down the heat to medium-low and simmer on the stove for about 1½ hours or until the meat is tender.

3. Add the potatoes, carrots, onions, mushrooms, and celery. Bring to a boil again, cover partially, and simmer for 45 minutes. (The stew can be cooled at this point and refrigerated. Bring it to room temperature and reheat when ready to serve.)

4. Check stew for salt, flavor, and thickness. Boil down if necessary and/or thicken with cornstarch mixed with 2 tablespoons water. Serve sprinkled with parsley.

Prep time: 45 minutes
Cooking time: 2 1/2 hours
Serves 6-8

HANUKKAH BRISKET

Say it with me: Classic. Jewish. Recipe. For non-Jews out there, think of this as an exceptionally flavorful pot roast. I make brisket every year and serve it with fried potato latkes. Recently I made a tremendous leftover discovery—on the day after your brisket party, slice leftovers into small pieces and serve as a meat sauce on spaghetti. Genius.

2 teaspoons paprika
1 teaspoon dry mustard
Salt and freshly ground black pepper
2 tablespoons extra virgin olive oil
5–6 pound brisket
2 onions, peeled and coarsely chopped
4–5 cloves garlic, peeled and crushed
2 carrots, peeled and coarsely chopped
2 stalks celery, coarsely chopped
4 sprigs parsley
3 bay leaves
1 6-ounce can tomato paste
1 1/2 cups tomato sauce
2 cups beef stock
1 cup red wine
1/2 cup soy sauce
1 14-ounce can diced tomatoes

1. Preheat oven to 325 degrees.
2. In a small bowl, combine the paprika, mustard, salt and pepper, and olive oil. Rub over the meat and let it rest while you prepare the vegetables.
3. Place the onions, garlic, carrots, celery, parsley and bay leaves in the bottom of a Dutch oven. Place the brisket on top of the vegetables.

4. In a large bowl combine the tomato paste, tomato sauce, beef stock, red wine, soy sauce and diced tomatoes. Pour over brisket.

5. Cover Dutch oven and roast for about 3 hours. A fork should penetrate pretty easily. Remove lid and roast 30 minutes more.

6. Remove meat from oven; cool. Remove meat from pot. Slice meat across the grain and place in a 9 x 13-inch roasting pan. Cool the sauce and vegetables in the refrigerator. Once cool, remove the congealed fat. Process the sauce and the vegetables in a food processor, or with an immersion blender, adding stock if needed. Pour over meat. Cover and refrigerate until ready to serve.

7. Reheat, covered with foil, in a 325-degree oven for 30 minutes.

Prep time: 30 minutes
Cooking time: 3 1/2 hours
Serves 10-12 people for dinner, and 20 as part of a holiday potluck

BRISKET WITH PRUNES

This is a wonderful springtime brisket. Onions, prunes, and orange marmalade are easy to keep in the house, as is beer, which makes a fine slow-cooking liquid.

2 onions, peeled and sliced
1 5-pound lean brisket
1 12-ounce can beer
1 cup beef broth
1/4 cup soy sauce
2 cups dried pitted prunes
1 tablespoon brown sugar
2 tablespoons orange marmalade (preferably bitter)
1 tablespoon brandy
Zest and juice of 1 lemon
1 1/2 teaspoons ground ginger
1 teaspoon cinnamon
1 tablespoon Worcestershire sauce
Freshly ground black pepper, to taste

1. Preheat oven to 350 degrees. Tear a piece of heavy-duty aluminum foil large enough to wrap the brisket and onions. Sprinkle half the onions over foil. Set the brisket on top of the onions. Place the remaining onions on top of the brisket. Seal tightly and place the wrapped meat in a Dutch oven, and cover. Roast 2 hours. Discard foil.
2. Meanwhile, combine the remaining ingredients in a large saucepan and bring to a boil over medium-high heat. Remove from heat. Pour over brisket in Dutch oven. Reduce heat to 300, cover pot and roast for 1 more hour.
3. Remove the pot from the oven. Remove the meat, slice it against the grain, and cover it with the sauce.

Prep time: 25 minutes. Cooking time: 3–4 hours. Serves 6–8.

STEAK WITH RED WINE BUTTER SAUCE

Talk about classic steakhouse delicacies... there's nothing like steak with a flavored butter sauce. The French make béarnaise sauce, which is terrific and not at all difficult. But this sauce is even easier and more nuanced, plus the robust flavor of the reduced red wine is divine.

1 cup dry red wine
1/2 cup orange juice
1/4 cup balsamic vinegar
1 teaspoon tomato paste
1/3 cup minced shallots
1/2 cup (1 stick) unsalted butter
Salt and freshly ground black pepper, to taste
4 8-ounce steaks of your choice

1. In a small heavy saucepan, combine the first 5 ingredients and boil the mixture down over medium high heat until it is quite thick, 15-25 minutes depending on the size of the pan. Keep an eye on it near the end—you want a viscous but not dry consistency.
2. Off the heat, with a whisk, beat in the butter 1 tablespoon at a time. Adjust the seasonings. Pour into serving bowl.
3. You can serve the sauce right away, or leave it out at room temperature. If you refrigerate it, let it soften at room temperature before serving. (If you try to heat it up, it will separate. If this happens, let it cool to room temperature and whisk it again.)
4. Grill or sauté the steaks to your liking and serve with the butter.

Total time: 40 minutes
Serves 4

Lamb

LAZY LAMB CHOPS
CURRY MUSTARD LAMB CHOPS
MARINATED BUTTERFLIED LEG OF LAMB
LAMB TAGINE WITH COUSCOUS
LEG OF LAMB WITH MUSTARD CRUST

LAZY LAMB CHOPS

Broiled lamb chops are the ultimate lazy meal. When I was young they sold shoulder chops that were hard to cut. Now it is very easy to buy thick cuts with just a little T-bone in them. I like this marinade, but you could just as easily sprinkle with salt and pepper and broil.

6 cloves garlic, peeled
2 tablespoons rosemary leaves
1 tablespoon salt
Several turns freshly ground black pepper
2 tablespoons extra virgin olive oil
Juice of 1 lemon
4 regular or 8 small thick-cut lamb chops

1. In a small food processor or by hand, mince the garlic and rosemary with the salt. Add pepper, olive oil and lemon juice. Rub the mixture all over the lamb chops. Marinate 15 minutes or overnight.
2. For thick chops: In a broiler, on a grill, or in a sauté pan, cook the chops over medium-high heat for 5 minutes. Turn and cook another 5 minutes. Turn heat to low and cook 5 more minutes. The chops should be perfectly medium. Thinner chops cook faster.

Prep time: 5 minutes
Marinating time: 15 minutes or overnight
Cooking time: 15 minutes
Serves 4

CURRY MUSTARD LAMB CHOPS

There is nothing lazier than sprinkling meat with a few spices, painting the surface with mustard, and broiling till done. So if you ever thought lamb was too much work, think again, and start impressing people (or yourself) the lazy way. This recipe has strong flavors, which I love.

8 small lamb chops, around 1-1/2 inch thick
Salt and freshly ground black pepper, to taste
2 teaspoons curry powder
2 tablespoons Dijon mustard

1. Sprinkle lamb chops with salt and pepper, and then with curry powder. (The amount of curry powder you'll need may vary depending on the surface area of the chops.)
2. Preheat broiler.
3. Put mustard in a small bowl. Paint the top side of the chops with some mustard. Place the lamb on broiler pan lined with foil, and broil 4 inches from the heat source until the mustard is brown, 5 minutes. Turn over and paint the other side with mustard. Broil until brown, 5 minutes. Turn off the broiler, turn the oven to 350 degrees, and cook chops until done, another 5 minutes or less depending on your taste.

Prep time: 5 minutes
Cooking time: 15-20 minutes
Serves 4

MARINATED BUTTERFLIED LEG OF LAMB

Leg of lamb may sound very Henry VIII, but if Henry VIII knew how easy this recipe was, he probably would have executed fewer wives out of respect for their culinary efficiency. There are just three steps: Blend the marinade. Marinate the meat. Bake with no fuss, and serve. Lazy central, no matter what the century. This marinade was inspired by Craig Claiborn.

3 cloves peeled garlic
1 tablespoon salt
25 turns freshly ground black pepper
3 bay leaves
1 1/2 teaspoons powdered ginger
1 1/2 teaspoons dried sage
1 1/2 teaspoons dried marjoram
3 tablespoons soy sauce
3 tablespoons extra virgin olive oil
5-pound leg of lamb, butterflied

1. Drop the garlic into the blender while it is running, to mince. With the blender off, add the salt and pepper, bay leaves, ginger, sage, marjoram, soy sauce, and oil. Process.
2. Place lamb in large plastic bag and cover with marinade. Marinate overnight.
3. Bake at 350 degrees, or barbecue over indirect heat, for 45 minutes. (Cook to 135 degrees for medium rare.) Let rest 10 minutes. Slice and serve.

Prep time for marinade: 10 minutes
Marinating time: Overnight
Cooking time: 45 minutes
Serves 8-10

LAMB TAGINE WITH COUSCOUS

No need to brown the meat in this lazy stew. Combine all ingredients, cook, stir, and cook some more. This is another make-in-advance recipe. Josie is a big proponent of cooking mass amounts of food on Sunday, freezing in batches, and reheating during the work week. This recipe suits a make-ahead cooking style like hers. (I know there are a lot of ingredients, but they are staples and should be on hand.)

3 pounds boneless leg of lamb, cut into 2-inch pieces
4 cloves garlic, peeled
1-inch piece of ginger, sliced
1 1/2 teaspoons salt
1/8 teaspoon red pepper flakes
1/2 teaspoon imported Spanish paprika (it has a smoky flavor)
1/2 teaspoon paprika
1 1/2 teaspoons ground cumin
1/4 teaspoon cinnamon
1 medium onion, thinly sliced, divided
1 14-ounce can diced tomatoes, undrained
1 1/2 cup chicken stock
1/3 cup orange juice
2 tablespoons honey
Pinch of saffron
2 cups peeled carrots, cut into 1/2-inch pieces
1 cup celery, sliced into 1/2-inch pieces
1/2 preserved lemon peel in 1/4-inch julienne, or 1 fresh Meyer
    lemon cut into 1/4-inch slices
1 cup pitted Kalamata olives, quartered
1 cup couscous
1/4 cup sliced almonds

1 tablespoon butter
1 1/2 tablespoons sesame seeds
1/3 cup minced cilantro leaves and tender stems

1. Preheat oven to 325 degrees. Put meat in a large heavy stew casserole or Dutch oven. Combine garlic, ginger, and other spices in small food processor, and process to mince the garlic and ginger. Add half the onion slices and pulse to roughly chop. Combine the mixture with the meat in the Dutch oven.
2. Place the Dutch oven over high heat and cook, turning meat frequently, about 3 minutes, until the spices release their aroma.
3. In a medium bowl combine the tomatoes, chicken stock, orange juice, honey and saffron. Pour the mixture over the lamb. Bring to a boil and then turn down to a simmer. Cover the meat with the other half of the sliced onions, cover the pot, and transfer to oven to braise for 1 hour.
4. Add carrots, celery, olives and lemons or preserved lemons. Cover and braise for another 1 hour. (At this point, the lamb can be set aside to cool and then refrigerated. Reheat in a low oven.)
5. To serve, prepare the couscous according to the package directions. Sauté almonds in butter and when they start to brown, add the sesame seeds. Pour the mixture over couscous. Garnish both stew and couscous with cilantro.

Prep time: 30 minutes
Cooking time: 2 hours
Serves 6

LEG OF LAMB WITH MUSTARD CRUST

The credit for this simple technique goes to Julia Child. Don't let the long cooking time put you off. The minimal ingredients, one pot cooking style and elegant presentation are worth every moment that you'll spend on your couch, reading, while your leg of lamb cooks.

1 clove garlic, peeled
1 slice of fresh ginger, peeled
1 tablespoon minced fresh rosemary
1/2 cup Dijon mustard
2 tablespoons soy sauce
4 tablespoons extra virgin olive oil
1 6-pound leg of lamb on the bone, with the H-bone cut out (your
    butcher can do this for you)
1 cup beef stock

1. Preheat oven to 350 degrees.
2. In a small food processor or blender, chop the garlic, ginger, and rosemary. Add the mustard and soy sauce. Blend in olive oil, a tablespoon at a time, so it forms an emulsion. Set aside.
3. Paint lamb with Dijon mixture, reserving 2 tablespoons.
4. Roast lamb about 1¼ hours until it reaches 135 degrees for medium-rare.
5. Remove lamb from roasting pan. Let it rest 10 minutes. Pour out fat from roasting pan. Put roasting pan on the stove top, add 1 cup beef stock and boil down for 5 minutes until reduced slightly. Off heat, add the remaining 2 tablespoons of Dijon mixture.
6. Slice lamb and serve, passing sauce separately.

Prep time: 15 minutes
Cooking time: 2 hours
Serves 6-8

Pork

PORK TENDERLOIN WITH CHILI MARINADE
PORK TENDERLOIN WITH BALSAMIC MARINADE
PORK WITH SPANISH PAPRIKA
PRECOOKED PORK TENDERLOIN

PORK TENDERLOIN WITH CHILI MARINADE

Pork tenderloin is doubly lazy because it takes beautifully both to marinades and quick-fire cooking methods like broiling or grilling. Since pork tenderloin can dry out so easily, invest in a meat thermometer and rely on it to hit 140 degrees to tell you when the meat is done. No thinking required.

1 teaspoon Thai red chili paste
1/2 cup orange juice
Juice of 1 lemon
3 tablespoons brown sugar
1/4 cup ketchup
1 1/2 teaspoons ground cumin
2 pork tenderloins, around 1 pound each

1. Combine all ingredients except pork in a medium bowl. Put pork in a zip lock bag. Pour the marinade over and let marinate in refrigerator at least 30 minutes (overnight is better).
2. Preheat the broiler. Remove the pork from the marinade and place it on a foil-lined broiler pan. Set the broiler pan on a rack so the pork is 4 inches from the broiler, and broil 5 minutes. Turn the pork; broil 5 more minutes. Turn off the broiler, turn the oven to 350 degrees, and cook pork 5-10 more minutes (check with meat thermometer partway through). Once meat reaches 140 degrees, remove from oven and let rest 5 minutes before cutting. (Or grill the tenderloin using a similar technique: 5 minutes per side on the flame, and 5-10 minutes indirect heat.)
3. Slice and serve.

Prep time: 10 minutes
Marinating time: 30 minutes to several days
Cooking time: 20 minutes
Serves 4-6

PORK TENDERLOIN WITH BALSAMIC MARINADE

Rosemary is one of the easiest herbs to grow, whether you live in frigid Chicago or sunny California. With a pot of rosemary on your windowsill, this recipe becomes a hate-to-shop-gourmand's dream. Either keep the pork tenderloins frozen and in the house, or pick them up at the store as needed.

1/4 cup olive oil
1/4 cup soy sauce
1/4 cup balsamic vinegar
1 tablespoon grainy mustard
4-6 cloves garlic, peeled and pressed
1 tablespoon chopped rosemary
2 pork tenderloins, around 1 pound each

1. In a small bowl or measuring cup, combine all ingredients except pork. Put the tenderloins in a zip lock bag. Pour the marinade over and let marinate in refrigerator 1 hour or overnight.
2. Preheat the broiler. Remove the pork from the marinade and place on a foil-lined broiler pan. Broil 4 inches from the broiler for 5 minutes. Turn the pork; broil 5 more minutes. Turn off the broiler, turn the oven to 350 degrees, and cook pork 5-10 more minutes (check with meat thermometer partway through). Once meat reaches 140 degrees, remove from oven and let rest 5 minutes before cutting. (Or grill the tenderloin using a similar technique: 5 minutes per side on the flame, and 5-10 minutes indirect heat.)

Prep time: 5 minutes
Marinating time: 1 hour to several days
Cooking time: 20 minutes
Serves 4-6

PORK WITH SPANISH PAPRIKA

Not all marinades are wet ones. Dry rubs and pastes also pack a hefty wallop in flavor when smeared on meat and allowed to marinate. After that, this recipe is a lazy case of slice and sauté.

5 cloves garlic, peeled
1/4 cup minced fresh oregano leaves, or 2 tablespoons dried
    oregano
2 teaspoons fresh thyme leaves, or 1 teaspoon dried thyme
1 tablespoon imported Spanish paprika (it has a smoky flavor)
1 teaspoon salt
20 turns freshly ground black pepper
1 tablespoon red wine vinegar
2-4 tablespoons extra virgin olive oil
2 pounds pork tenderloin

1. In a small food processor, mince the garlic. Add the 6 next ingredients and 2 tablespoons of the olive oil. Process until a paste forms.
2. Rub the paste onto the tenderloin, wrap in plastic wrap, and marinate overnight.
3. Discard plastic wrap and slice the tenderloin into ¾-inch slices. Heat the remaining 2 tablespoons of olive oil in a large sauté pan. Brown slices on both sides over medium-high heat and reduce the heat to medium to cook until done, 10-15 minutes. You may need to do this in batches, adding more oil to the pan if necessary.

Prep time: 10 minutes
Marinating time: 24 hours
Cooking time: 20 minutes
Serves 4-6

PRECOOKED PORK TENDERLOIN

This way of cooking pork tenderloin is from Mark Bittman of the the *New York Times*. It is so ingenious I'm amazed it hasn't been repeated more often. The advantage for the lazy gourmet is that you don't have to plan in advance. You don't marinate, you just cook. And it's good.

1 tablespoon extra virgin olive oil
1–1 1/2 pounds pork tenderloin
Salt and freshly ground black pepper
1 tablespoon butter
1/2 cup water, white wine, or chicken stock
1/4 cup cream
1 tablespoon Dijon mustard

1. In a large nonstick sauté pan, heat oil on medium-high heat and when shimmering, add pork tenderloin (you may have to curve it to fit in the pan). Use tongs to turn the meat to cook it on all sides, around 5 minutes. Remove pork from pan and turn off the heat.
2. Off the heat, sprinkle the pork with salt and pepper and cut into 1-inch slices. At this point, you can wait a half hour or so to finish the dish. When you are ready, turn the heat to medium, add butter to the pan. When it is hot, add the meat slices. Cook the slices 2 minutes per side, or until cooked through. Remove pork to a plate and keep warm.
3. To the pan add ½ cup liquid, turn up the heat, and bring to a boil. Cook 2 minutes until liquid reduces by half. Turn down the heat, add the cream, and cook for 2 minutes. Stir in mustard. Cook until the sauce has thickened. Check the seasonings and add more salt and pepper if it needs it. This makes about ⅓ cup of sauce. Serve pork with sauce.

Total time: 30 minutes
Serves 2–3

Desserts and Cookies

PURE CHOCOLATE
COOKIES
FRUIT

When I first started cooking, I dabbled exclusively in desserts. Complicated, multi-step, non-lazy desserts—chocolate soufflé, chocolate mousse cake, three-flavor cheesecake, profiteroles, mint Bavarian with chocolate sauce... but now I frequent pastry shops and indulge only in lazy desserts.

Drop-dead-lazy requires zero cooking—ice cream purchased directly from the store. To enhance the basics, you can branch out with Clara's Hot Fudge (page 156) or Helen's Bananas Foster (page 173), both of which can be pulled together in 5 minutes.

The rest of the desserts in this sweetly lazy chapter are divided into three basic food groups: Chocolate, Cookies, and Fruit.

Pure Chocolate

ALICE'S POTS DE CRÈME
CLARA'S HOT FUDGE
FRENCH CHOCOLATE CAKE
CHOCOLATE MOUSSE CAKE
HOT CHOCOLATE CAKES
UNBELIEVABLY GOOD BROWNIES
CREAM CHEESE BROWNIES

You know you're raising a child with a skewed sense of reality when she comes back dazed after a play date, bearing the news that "Morgan's house doesn't have a chocolate shelf." Our household chocolate shelf isn't just for chocolate chips. We store unsweetened chocolate from two different countries and bittersweet chocolate from three. Semisweet chocolate chips are a given, but I also have bars of varying levels of sweetness, powders, and the occasional box of straight-up truffles. Josie thinks I'm a bit snobby about my consumption and advocates purchasing your chocolate at Costco where 72 ounces of Toll House morsels are sold at a compelling price point. However (and wherever) you shop, the bottom line is that no kitchen should be so devoid of chocolate that it is impossible to whip up an emergency double batch of something chocolate—in whatever form it takes.

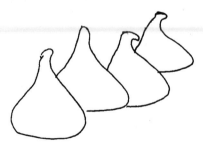

ALICE'S POTS DE CRÈME

In the early 1970s there was a lot of pot going around, but what I cared about was pots de crème. Cousin Alice gave me this recipe over 30 years ago when her girls were preteens and mine were non-existent. It is a vastly simplified version of a famous French custard recipe and while it does need to be made in advance, it is extraordinarily easy.

3/4 cup whole or 2% milk
1 cup semisweet or bittersweet chocolate chips
1 egg
1 teaspoon vanilla
2 tablespoons granulated sugar
Pinch of salt
1 tablespoon flavored liquor or 1 teaspoon instant decaffeinated coffee (optional)
Whipped cream, for garnish (optional)

1. Heat milk just to boiling in a small saucepan or in the microwave.
2. While milk heats, put all the other ingredients in the blender.
3. Add the hot milk to the blender and blend at low speed for at least a minute, until the mixture is perfectly smooth. Pour into 4 individual ramekins.
4. Chill at least 2 hours. Garnish with whipped cream, if desired.

Prep time: 7 minutes
Chilling time: 2 hours
Serves 4

CLARA'S HOT FUDGE

My girls sometimes tease me that I've ruined them as artists because they had such a stable childhood. Perhaps their memory is different than mine—I can remember Josie running away to Yosemite (although, okay, I went with her). Meanwhile Molly never got into any trouble at all—and that just isn't normal. But when they reprimand me for parental stability, all I can think is, it's all thanks to the hot fudge. Our finest family moments were spent in front of the fireplace with a Scrabble board, pouring hot fudge straight from the pot. Being lazy of course, you'll want to buy (not make) the ice cream.

4 tablespoons (1/2 stick) unsalted butter
2 ounces unsweetened chocolate
2 1/4 cups powdered sugar
1/2 cup whole or 2% milk
1 teaspoon vanilla

1. Melt butter and chocolate together in small heavy bottomed saucepan over low flame. (Some people would use a double boiler, but I think if you keep the flame low and watch it, butter and chocolate can be melted on the stovetop with less fuss.)
2. Over medium heat, add some of the sugar and then some of the milk, stirring after each addition, and continue alternating until both are used up. Cook at a gentle boil for 3-4 minutes, until thickened.
3. Off the heat, stir in vanilla.

Total time: 10 minutes
Makes 1 cup

FRENCH CHOCOLATE CAKE

Count them: Four ingredients. Four. You will not believe how amazing this cake is.

3/4 cup (1 1/2 sticks) unsalted butter
8 ounces bittersweet chocolate, cut into 1-ounce pieces (Molly prefers Callebaut)
1 cup granulated sugar
6 eggs

1. Preheat oven to 325 degrees. Put a kettle of water on to boil (this is for the bain marie, step 5 below).
2. Melt butter and chocolate together in a large glass bowl in the microwave (5 minutes at 50% power). Whisk to combine, and set aside to cool 5 minutes.
3. Spray a 9-inch round cake pan with oil spray, cover the bottom with parchment paper cut to fit, and spray again.
4. Whisk the sugar into the chocolate mixture. Add the eggs, one at a time, whisking well after each addition. Pour mixture into prepared pan.
5. Cook cake in a bain marie: Place the cake pan in a larger ovenproof pan. Pour hot water from the kettle into the larger pan so it reaches halfway up the sides of the smaller pan. Bake 50 minutes. Remove from oven, remove smaller pan from larger pan, and cool on a wire rack before unmolding.
6. Serve with Raspberry Sauce (see next page) and whipped cream.

Prep time: 20 minutes
Cooking time: 50 minutes
Serves 8-10

RASPBERRY SAUCE

1/4 cup granulated sugar
1 12-ounce bag of raspberries, thawed

1. In a small sauce pan, heat sugar and 2 tablespoons of water over medium heat until just melted. Cool.
2. Put thawed raspberries in a food processor. Add melted cooled sugar and process until well combined. Strain the sauce to get out seeds. Serve at room temperature.

Total time: 15 minutes
Makes about 1 cup

CHOCOLATE MOUSSE CAKE

This recipe is a best friend's best friend, as in you should distribute it when someone you adore is in deep personal crisis. With the same ingredients as the French Chocolate Cake (page 157), the melted sugar makes the consistency extra smooth.

1 cup granulated sugar
1/2 cup water
1/2 cup (1 stick) unsalted butter, cut in 4 pieces
8 ounces bittersweet chocolate, chopped
6 eggs

1. Preheat oven to 325 degrees.
2. In a heavy saucepan, over medium heat, cook sugar and water together until the sugar dissolves (the liquid will look clear). Then add butter and heat until melted. Off heat, add chocolate and stir until the chocolate melts. Cool 5 minutes.
3. While the chocolate is cooling, spray an 8-inch round cake pan with oil spray, line with parchment cut to fit the pan, and spray again. The cake rises high while it bakes and it needs the deeper pan. If you don't have one, use a 9-inch round cake pan.
4. To the cooled chocolate mixture, add the eggs, one by one, whisking well. Pour the batter into the prepared pan.
5. Place the cake pan in a larger ovenproof pan. Bring a kettle of water to a boil. Pour hot water from the kettle into the larger pan so it reaches halfway up the sides of the smaller pan. Bake 40 minutes. Remove from oven, remove smaller pan from larger pan, and cool on a wire rack before unmolding. Serve with whipped cream, coffee ice cream, or Raspberry Sauce (see previous page) and vanilla ice cream.

Prep time: 20 minutes
Cooking time: 40 minutes
Serves 8–10

HOT CHOCOLATE CAKES

Batter for these chocolate cakes can and should be made at least one day in advance. On the evening they're being served, scoop the batter into ramekins. Sixteen minutes before serving, tuck them into the oven. When you serve delectable warm chocolate cake right after dinner, people will think you're a genius. And this is before they've tasted it. Since the main ingredient is chocolate, be sure to use a high-quality brand.

8 ounces bittersweet chocolate, chopped
3/4 cup (1 1/2 sticks) unsalted butter, cut into 6 chunks
1 cup granulated sugar
3 1/2 tablespoons cornstarch
Pinch of salt
4 eggs
4 egg yolks

1. Make the batter: melt together chocolate and butter in microwave (5 minutes at 50% power) or in a double boiler. Let the chocolate mixture cool a little.
2. In a small bowl, combine sugar, cornstarch, and salt.
3. In another bowl, with a whisk, beat together eggs and egg yolks.
4. With a wooden spoon, stir the sugar mixture into the chocolate. Then beat in the eggs. Refrigerate the mixture overnight.
5. At least 30 minutes before serving, preheat the oven to 400 degrees. Spray 8 1-cup ramekins with oil spray. Fill the ramekins less than half full of chocolate mixture. Place ramekins on a cookie sheet. You can leave the filled ramekins out for an hour or so if you need to. Bake for 16 minutes. The cakes should be just set in the middle.
6. Serve right away with a scoop of ice cream on top.

Prep time: 15 minutes. Waiting time: 6–24 hours.
Cooking time: 16 minutes. Serves 8.

UNBELIEVABLY GOOD BROWNIES

When the Lazy Gourmet gives a chocolate recipe that is a little more time consuming than the classic box brownie recipe, you know it's for a good reason. In this case, the reason is the texture. Try it. It is fudgy but light, rich but not cloying. The recipe is based on one by Nick Malgieri that I found in the *New York Times*.

1/2 cup (1 stick) unsalted butter
4 ounces bittersweet chocolate, cut in 1-ounce pieces
2 eggs
Pinch of salt
1/2 cup dark brown sugar
1/2 cup granulated sugar
1 teaspoon vanilla
1/2 cup all-purpose flour

1. Preheat oven to 350 degrees. Spray an 8 x 8-inch square cake pan with oil spray, line bottom with parchment cut to fit, and spray again.
2. In a glass bowl, melt butter and chocolate in microwave (4 minutes at 50% power) or melt in a double boiler. Cool 5 minutes.
3. In a medium bowl, whisk together eggs, salt, both sugars, and vanilla until light and bubbly. Whisk in chocolate mixture. Fold in flour. Pour into pan.
4. Bake 25-30 minutes, until the top is shiny and beginning to crack.
5. Cool on wire rack, or use the Alice Medrich method for cooling brownies: put the pan right from the oven into the freezer for 5 minutes. This stops the cooking and maintains a creamier consistency. After 5 minutes, cool the brownies on a cooling rack and when cool, cut into squares.

Prep time: 15 minutes. Cooking time: 25 minutes.
Makes 9 large brownies.

CREAM CHEESE BROWNIES

I've been making a version of cream cheese brownies for years. Recently, I have been hankering for less cakey cream cheese brownies, so I've been experimenting. This recipe is the glorious result.

For the brownies:
 3 ounces unsweetened chocolate
 1/2 cup (1 stick) unsalted butter
 1 1/4 cups granulated sugar
 Pinch of salt
 1 teaspoon vanilla
 3 eggs
 1/2 cup all-purpose flour
For the cheesecake:
 12 ounces cream cheese (low-fat is ok)
 3/4 cup granulated sugar
 3 eggs
 3/4 teaspoon vanilla
 1 1/2 tablespoons all-purpose flour

1. Preheat oven to 325 degrees. Line a 9 x 13-inch glass baking pan with foil, with some overhang over the sides (this is to facilitate cutting after brownies bake). Spray the foil with oil spray. Set aside.
2. Place chocolate and butter in a large glass bowl. Microwave 5 minutes at 50% power. Stir with a whisk and set aside to cool 5 minutes. Then stir in the sugar, salt, and vanilla, and then the eggs, one by one. Fold in the flour. Reserve 1 tablespoon of the brownie mixture in a little bowl. Pour the rest into the prepared pan, spreading it with the back of the spoon to fill the whole pan.
3. While the chocolate is melting and then cooling, make the cheesecake: Put the cream cheese in the food processor and process to soften. Add the sugar and process well, scraping down the sides of the bowl. Add the vanilla. Add the eggs, one by one, and then

the flour. Pulse once or twice more to incorporate the flour. Take 1 tablespoon of the cream cheese mixture and add it to the reserved tablespoon of the brownie mixture.

4. Pour the cheesecake mixture gently over the brownie mixture already in the pan. (You're trying to make a flat layer.)

5. In the little bowl, stir together the 2 tablespoons of brownie-cheese cake mixture. Scoop the mixture into a little sandwich bag and squeeze it into the corner. Snip off $^1/_{16}$-inch from the corner. Pipe chocolate mixture into four or five parallel rows the length of the pan. Then gently run a knife down the short end every 2 inches. This makes a design on top of the cake.

6. Bake 40-50 minutes, or until the cheese layer is set and a little brown around the edges. Remove pan from the oven and place it directly in the freezer for 15 minutes. (This is an Alice Medrich trick and makes the brownies very creamy.) Afterwards, cool on a wire rack and then refrigerate before cutting.

Prep time: 15 minutes
Cooking time: 40 minutes
Makes 32 smallish brownies or 24 large ones,
depending how you cut them

Cookies

CHOCOLATE CHIP COOKIES EXTRAORDINAIRE
CROQ-TÉLÉ COOKIES
PECAN SHORTBREAD COOKIES
BROWN SUGAR SHORTBREAD
MATZOH CRUNCH
CHOCOLATE-TOFFEE BARS

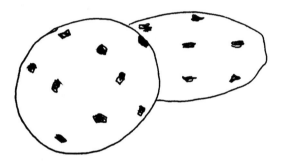

CHOCOLATE CHIP COOKIES EXTRAORDINAIRE

Sometimes I wonder if my family loves me for me or for these cookies. My first son-in-law used to get terribly hurt if I didn't bring him cookies when I visited Chicago, and my second son-in-law eats them two at a time from the freezer where I keep them to extend their shelf life. Unlike chewy chocolate chip cookies, these have a bit more flour and firmer texture. They really do take well to the freezer, provided they're sealed from freezer burn in gallon bags. The idea of using twice as much white sugar as brown sugar (instead of equal amounts) came from Jane Benet, who wrote for the *San Francisco Chronicle* over 30 years ago.

1 cup (2 sticks) unsalted butter, softened
1/2 cup golden brown sugar, packed
1 cup granulated sugar
1 1/2 teaspoons vanilla
2 eggs
2 1/3 cups all-purpose flour
1 teaspoon baking soda
1/2 teaspoon salt
3 cups (18 ounces) semisweet chocolate chips (I prefer Ghirardelli)

1. Preheat oven to 350 degrees. Line 2 cookie sheets with parchment.
2. Cream butter with both sugars until light and fluffy (this is easier in a heavy-duty mixer). Beat in vanilla and eggs until smooth. Put flour in mixer bowl and add baking soda and salt on top of flour. Stir to combine. Stir in chocolate chips.
3. Drop dough in heaping tablespoons onto cookie sheets. (You can also use a 1½-tablespoon ice cream scoop for more uniform size.) Bake 15 minutes, switching pans after 10 minutes. The finished cookies should be a little bit dark on top to get the real caramelized flavor. Cool on a wire rack.

Prep time: 15 minutes. Cooking time: 15 minutes. Makes 4 dozen cookies.

CROQ-TÉLÉ COOKIES

This cookie is based on a cookie made in Paris by Patisserie Arnaud Larher in the Montmartre District. Various versions have appeared on the Internet, some with the original metric weights for the ingredients. This is my simplified, but still delicious, version. The cookie is sweet but slightly salty.

3/4 cup hazelnuts, lightly toasted and skinned
1/2 cup granulated sugar
1 cup all-purpose flour
A smidge less than 1/2 teaspoon fleur de sel or Kosher salt
1/2 cup (1 stick) cold unsalted butter, diced

1. Preheat oven to 350 degrees. Line 2 cookie sheets with parchment paper.
2. Place hazelnuts and sugar in food processor. Pulse until finely ground, around 1 minute. Turn out mixture onto wax paper. Set aside.
3. Place flour and salt in food processor. Pulse once or twice to combine. Add diced butter and pulse until mixture is sandy in texture. Add nut mixture and pulse until clumps form.
4. Shape dough into pieces around the size of cherries and form it to look like a Hershey's Kiss with a point at the top. Place chunks an inch or so apart on cookie sheets. Bake around 15 minutes, switching cookie sheets or turning them around halfway through, until lightly colored. Remove sheets from oven and let rest a couple of minutes. Cool on wire rack.

Prep time: 20 minutes
Cooking time: 15 minutes
Makes around 3 dozen cookies

PECAN SHORTBREAD COOKIES

Pecan shortbread is a new addition to my repertoire. Not that I ever get tired of chocolate, but sometimes it's nice to bake up a cookie that has none—just for variety's sake. An advantage of this particularly quick and easy recipe is that you can keep the dough in the freezer or in the refrigerator and bake as needed. It's a much fresher approach to convenience cooking than those horrible processed logs of store-bought cookie dough.

1 cup pecans, lightly toasted
2 1/8 cups all-purpose flour
1 cup confectioner's sugar
Pinch of salt
1 cup (2 sticks) unsalted butter, at room temperature
1 teaspoon vanilla

1. In food processor, chop the pecans until finely ground. Add flour, sugar, and salt and process until combined.
2. Add butter and vanilla to processor. Process just until dough forms.
3. Drape a 7½ x 3½ x 2½-inch loaf pan with plastic wrap. (This will make the dough easier to remove from the pan.) Pack the dough in and smooth the top. Cover tightly with plastic wrap. Refrigerate at least 8 hours, or up to several days.
4. When ready to cook, preheat oven to 350 degrees. Line cookie sheets with parchment paper. Remove cookie dough from the loaf pan. Cut it in half lengthwise and slice each half into ¼-inch slices. Place them on cookie sheets, about an inch apart. Bake 15-20 minutes. They will be slightly colored.
5. Cool 30 seconds and transfer to wire rack.

Prep time: 20 minutes
Waiting time: 8 hours
Cooking time: 20 minutes
Makes 3 1/2 dozen cookies

BROWN SUGAR SHORTBREAD

A wonderful ice cream store in Berkeley (now sadly closed) made these and I thought they were so delicious I asked for the recipe. They gave it to me, albeit in a very large quantity. Since I can do math, below is a version for the average family.

Cooking spray
1/2 cup golden brown sugar
2 cups all-purpose flour
Pinch of salt
1/2 cup (1 stick) butter, softened and cut into 8 pieces
1 teaspoon vanilla
1 tablespoon brandy (optional)

1. Preheat the oven to 350 degrees. Spray an 8 x 8-inch square pan with oil spray.
2. In a food processor, process the sugar, flour, and salt together. Add the butter and process to form a dough. Add the vanilla and brandy and process.
3. Press the dough into the prepared pan; make sure it is flat. Make 6 cuts in the dough with a knife, 3 horizontal and 3 vertical (not all the way through), to divide the dough into 16 squares. Bake 45 minutes or until edges are firm and starting to brown.
4. Cool on a rack. Recut the cookies in the pan before you remove them.

Prep time: 10 minutes
Cooking time: 45 minutes
Makes 16 cookies

Matzoh Crunch

When Passover comes, since we can't eat leavened food products, chocolate chip cookies and brownies are out. This recipe is an excellent substitute. Matzoh Crunch is like English Toffee but even harder to mess up. The matzoh provides the crunch; all you need to provide is an eye on the sugar and butter so they don't burn.

3-4 pieces unsalted matzoh
1 cup (2 sticks) unsalted butter
1 cup brown sugar, all dark, all golden, or half and half, packed
1 cup semisweet or bittersweet chocolate chips
1/2 cup chopped hazelnuts, toasted and skinned

1. Preheat oven to 350 degrees. Line a 10 x 15-inch rimmed cookie sheet with foil and then cover with parchment. Cover the parchment with four matzoh. It doesn't matter if you have to break them into pieces to make them fit.
2. In a small saucepan over a medium-low flame, melt the butter and brown sugar together. Bring to a boil and simmer 3 minutes.
3. Pour the butter-sugar mixture over the matzoh and put in the oven. Cook 10-15 minutes, watching for burning (I put another cookie sheet on the oven shelf underneath the pan with the matzoh to help prevent burning).
4. Turn off the oven, sprinkle matzoh with chocolate chips, and put back in the oven for 4 minutes to melt the chips. Spread the melted chocolate over the matzoh with a spatula or the back of a spoon.
5. Sprinkle with chopped hazelnuts.
6. Place in the freezer for 15 minutes to harden the chocolate. Cut into pieces. The shapes will probably be irregular.

Total time: 25 minutes
Serves 8

CHOCOLATE-TOFFEE BARS

Worrying is the Jewish form of prayer, but even I can recognize that worrying 24/7 is a bit excessive—especially for a 7-year-old. When Josie was in 2nd grade, she had a steadily-growing clump of broken blood vessels under her eye, threatening to take over her face. Usually I'm not one to obsess over physical oddities, but this was bad. We signed her up for surgery and naturally, she worried. When the surgery didn't work and we had to do it again, she worried more. By the time the third surgery rolled around, I had come up with Worry Day. Worry Day is a beautiful time when all worries are condensed into one afternoon. For every worry you have, you get to eat a sweet. These toffee bars were a Worry Day favorite. At the time, the only challenge was finding the toffee bits at the store. Luckily, now that we're in the 21st century, they're available online. One less thing to worry about!

2 cups all-purpose flour
1 cup golden brown sugar, packed
Pinch of salt
1 cup (2 sticks) cold unsalted butter, sliced into small pieces
2 teaspoons vanilla
1 1/2 cup Ghirardelli Double Chocolate Chips (or another bittersweet chocolate chip)
1 cup Heath Bits 'O Brickle Toffee Bits (you can use sliced toasted almonds instead if you can't find the toffee)

1. Preheat the oven to 350 degrees. Line a 10 x 15-inch cookie sheet with sides with foil (this is to lift the dough out after it's done so it's easier to cut), and then cover with parchment paper.
2. Place flour, brown sugar, and salt in food processor. Pulse to combine. Add butter and vanilla and pulse until the butter is cut into little bits but has not started to clump into a dough. It will look very floury.

3. Pour dough into the pan and press flat (use a piece of wax paper and a flat pan or spatula to help flatten if necessary). Bake 20-25 minutes. The crust should be brown all over but not very dark. (It takes a little experience to get this just right.)

4. Sprinkle the crust with chocolate chips, as evenly as possible. Turn off oven and leave the pan in the oven 4 minutes. Spread chocolate mixture all over top of crust, using the back of a soup spoon. Sprinkle evenly with toffee bits or almonds. Place in the freezer for 15 minutes to harden the chocolate.

5. Lift the whole crust out of the pan and cut into squares.

Prep time: 15 minutes
Cooking time: 30 minutes
Makes 32-48 very rich bars

Fruit

HELEN'S BANANAS FOSTER
NECTARINE CRISP
PLUM TORTE
STRAWBERRIES WITH BALSAMIC VINEGAR

HELEN'S BANANAS FOSTER

Cousin Helen is known for her rolling laugh, her face-cracking smile, and her Bananas Foster. Last time I visited her in Florida I got to spend time with her daughter Heather as well. We were girls on the town, and while I won't fess up to going so far as to drink the Cointreau listed in this recipe, Helen's Bananas Foster is so lazy, three tipsy cousins can throw it together way past the witching hour.

3 tablespoons unsalted butter
1/4 cup golden brown sugar, packed
1/4 cup orange juice
1/4 teaspoon cinnamon
3 bananas, cut in 1/2-inch slices
3 tablespoons Cointreau (or any orange liqueur)

1. Melt sugar and butter together in a wide saucepan over medium heat. Add orange juice and cinnamon. Let it bubble a while.
2. Add bananas; cook 30 seconds. Add Cointreau and flame. Remove pan from heat and let cool down a couple of minutes.
3. Serve over vanilla ice cream or coffee ice cream.

Total time: 10 minutes
Serves 4

NECTARINE CRISP

My father could peel an apple in one long piece. For him, the whole thing just unraveled like a magic ribbon. Sometimes I worry that this is the only thing my girls will remember about their grandfather. They will wonder how a man like that produced a woman like me—because peeling fruit is not lazy. Fortunately, nectarines, unlike peaches, don't have to be peeled, so this recipe is super-lazy and still delicious enough that my father, the fruit fanatic, would have loved it.

For fruit mixture:
    4-5 nectarines, pitted and sliced 1/3 inch thick (about 6 cups)
    1/2 cup granulated sugar
    3 tablespoons all-purpose flour
    2 tablespoons lemon juice
    2 cups raspberries
For topping:
    1 cup all-purpose flour
    1 cup golden brown sugar, packed
    1/2 cup (1 stick) unsalted butter, at room temperature, cut into 1/2-inch pieces

1. Preheat oven to 375 degrees. Grease a 10-inch glass pie pan with butter or oil spray.
2. In a large bowl, toss the sliced the nectarines with sugar, flour, and lemon juice. Gently fold in raspberries and pour into pie pan.
3. In a food processor, process flour, and brown sugar. Add butter and pulse until mixture starts to hold together. Take a handful of the topping, squeeze it in your hand to combine, and place it on top of the fruit. Continue until all the topping is used. Sprinkle the last bits in the bare places. Bake on a cookie sheet (to catch any drips) for 45 minutes, until the topping is browned and the juices are bubbling. Serve warm with vanilla ice cream.

Prep time: 20 minutes. Cooking time: 45 minutes. Serves 8.

PLUM TORTE

As a mother, you never know what your kids are really up to in school. The first time I made this torte for my girls, Josie confessed that she didn't like plums because a boy from school spent recess throwing them at her from a plum tree on the playground. Molly never had that problem. If she had been on the playground, she would have organized a campaign to stop the plum thrower in his tracks. This is an old *New York Times* recipe, which was published so often that they don't publish it anymore.

1/2 cup (1 stick) unsalted butter, softened
3/4 cup granulated sugar
2 eggs
1 cup all-purpose flour
1 teaspoon baking powder
Pinch of salt
24 small Italian plums, halved; or 12 medium plums, halved;
    or 6 large plums, halved and each half cut in 4 slices
2 tablespoons granulated sugar
1 teaspoon cinnamon

1. Preheat oven to 350 degrees. Grease or oil spray the sides of a 9-inch springform pan. (You don't want to grease the bottom because you will be spreading the dough there and it needs to adhere a little.)
2. In an electric mixer or by hand, cream together butter and sugar until light. Add eggs and beat to combine. Add flour, baking powder, and salt. Mix until combined. Spoon dough into the prepared pan. It will be fairly stiff, so use a large spoon to spread it out.
3. Top the cake with the cut plums, skin side down and cut side up. Combine remaining sugar and cinnamon, and sprinkle on top.
4. Bake 50 minutes or until a toothpick placed in the center comes out clean. Serve warm or at room temperature with vanilla ice cream.

Prep time: 15 minutes. Cooking time: 50 minutes. Serves 8.

STRAWBERRIES WITH BALSAMIC VINEGAR

Strawberries with balsamic vinegar is another one of those gems that is less a recipe than a fine idea. The better the quality of the ingredients, the better the quality of the dessert.

2 cups strawberries, washed, hulled, and sliced
2 tablespoons granulated or golden brown sugar
1 teaspoon balsamic vinegar
Freshly ground black pepper

1. Sprinkle the strawberries with sugar, toss, and leave them to bleed (i.e. shed juice). They need at least 15 minutes, but can rest a couple of hours if need be (too long and they get mushy, though).
2. Toss mixture with vinegar and pepper. Taste and make adjustments.
3. Serve as is, or over vanilla ice cream.

Prep time: 10 minutes
Waiting time: 15 minutes
Serves 4

Tips and Tricks
from the Lazy Gourmet

Hate to shop? Hate to clean? Hate to cook after a long day? Whatever it is you despise, avoid it at all costs. Read on…

Imperishable Ingredients

Phooey on shopping. Use the ingredient lists in these recipes to build your monthly shopping list, and stock your kitchen with staples that take a very long time to go bad. Cooking when the cupboards are "bare" has never been so easy.

- Egg Soufflé (page 71)
- Penne with Simple Balsamic-Tomato Sauce (page 77)
- Fast Macaroni and Cheese (page 78)
- Asian Peanut-Sesame Noodles (page 81)
- Pea Soup (page 44)
- Red Lentil Soup (page 41)
- Bean and Corn Salad (page 32)
- Quinoa Pilaf with Garbanzo Beans (page 97)
- Clara's Hot Fudge (page 156)
- Helen's Banana's Foster (page 173)
- Chocolate Chip Cookies Extraordinaire (page 165)

One Dish Wonders

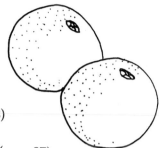

For cooks who hate to clean:
- Hummus (page 20)
- Alice's Gazpacho (page 38)
- Red Lentil Soup (page 41)
- Fast Macaroni and Cheese (page 78)
- Zucchini Couscous (page 98)
- Quinoa Pilaf with Garbanzo Beans (page 97)
- Easy Vegetarian Chili (page 65)
- Salmon or Tuna Piccata (page 100)
- Pan-Glazed Swordfish (page 104)
- Seared Tuna Pepper Steaks (page 107)
- Tuna, Languedoc Style (page 108)
- Crusty Scallops (page 113)
- Tarragon Garlic Chicken (page 116)
- Chicken with Sage and Wine (page 117)
- Turkey Balsamico (page 128)
- Turkey All'Arrabbiata (page 129)
- Curry Mustard Lamb Chops (page 142)
- Lamb Tagine (page 145)
- Precooked Pork Tenderloin (page 151)
- Alice's Pots de Crème (page 155)
- Clara's Hot Fudge (page 156)
- Helen's Banana's Foster (page 173)

Make Ahead Magic

No time today? Think ahead. The Lazy Gourmet adores anything that can be (briefly) prepared in advance and then baked, broiled, grilled or dressed whenever.

Sauces:
- Olive Vinaigrette (page 36): For chicken, chicken salad, vegetables or fish
- Basic Salad Dressing (page 28): For salad, chicken, vegetables or fish
- Mango Salsa (page 102): For chicken and fish
- Roasted Red Pepper Sauce (page 51): For artichokes or fish

Marinades:
- Cider Vinegar and Mustard Marinade (page 120): For chicken
- Cilantro Soy Marinade (page 109): For chicken or fish
- Sesame Teriyaki Marinade (page 133): For flank steak
- Chili Marinade (page 148): For pork
- Balsamic Marinade (page 149): For pork and chicken

Fancy Schmancy

Impress company or yourself by making these elegant meals in advance and then reheating or cooking without fuss while guests are in the house. This leaves you free to enjoy your evening out of the kitchen and apron free.
- Asparagus Soup (page 38)
- Roasted Carrot Soup (page 40)
- Curried Cauliflower Soup (page 42)
- Oven-Roasted Ratatouille (page 65)
- Penne Casserole with Two Cheeses (page 86)
- Salmon or Tuna Piccata (page 100)
- Halibut with Olive Paste and Pine Nut Crust (page 105)
- Chicken with Olives, Prunes, and Capers (page 127)
- Boeuf Bourguignon (page 137)
- Hanukkah Brisket (page 136)
- Brisket with Prunes (page 138)
- Marinated Butterflied Leg of Lamb (page 143)
- Lamb Tagine (page 145)
- Leg of Lamb with Mustard Crust (page 146)
- Pork Tenderloin with Chili Marinade (page 148)
- French Chocolate Cake (page 157)
- Unbelievably Good Brownies (page 161)
- Nectarine Crisp (page 174)
- Plum Torte (page 175)

Potluck Favorites

Not your average party fare... steal the show with these excellent shareables. They are ready to eat at room temperature, or serve cold.

- Mustard Gruyere Crackers (page 18)
- Blue Cheese ball (page 22)
- Uncle Harry's Chopped Liver (page 25)
- Prosciutto and Gruyère Pin wheels (page 26)
- Wild Rice and Smoked Chicken Salad (page 33)
- Farro, Tomato, and Mozzarella Salad (page 34)
- Chicken Salad with Olive Vinaigrette (page 36)
- Spicy Creamed Spinach (serve hot or warm) (page 62)
- Oven-Roasted Ratatouille (page 65)
- Quinoa Pilaf with Garbanzo Beans (page 97)
- Pasta Salad with Tomatoes, Broccoli, and Cheese (page 80)
- French Chocolate Cake (page 157)
- Cheesecake Brownies (page 162)
- Chocolate Chip Cookies (page 165)
- Matzoh Crunch (page 169)
- Nectarine Crisp (page 174)
- Plum Torte (page 175)

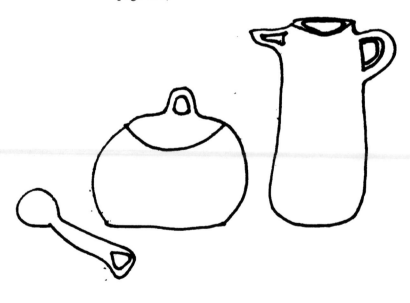

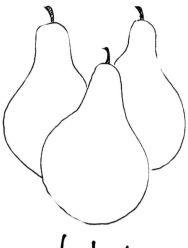

Index

Table of Equivalents

These are the most common equivalents for cooking in the American kitchen and are useful for doubling or halving recipes.

Dry and Liquid Measures

1/3 tablespoon	1 teaspoon	
1/2 tablespoon	1 1/2 teaspoons	
1 tablespoon	3 teaspoons	
1/8 cup	2 tablespoons	1 fluid ounce
1/4 cup	4 tablespoons	2 fluid ounces
1/3 cup	5 1/3 tablespoons	2+ fluid ounces
1/2 cup	8 tablespoons	4 fluid ounces
3/4 cup	12 tablespoons	6 fluid ounces
1 cup	16 tablespoons	8 fluid ounces
1 pint	2 cups	
1 quart	4 cups	
1 gallon	4 quarts	

Butter

1 pound	4 sticks	16 ounces	2 cups	
1/2 pound	2 sticks	8 ounces	1 cup	16 tablespoons
1/3 pound		5 1/3 ounces		11 tablespoons
1/4 pound	1 stick	4 ounces	1/2 cup	8 tablespoons
1/8 pound	1/2 stick	2 ounces	1/4 cup	4 tablespoons

Grated Cheddar Cheese (approximate)

1 pound	6 cups grated
8 ounces	2 cups grated
4 ounces	1 cup grated

Grated Gruyere Cheese (approximate)

4 ounces	1½ cups grated

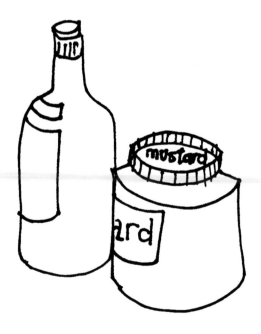

Acknowledgments

This book would never have been published were it not for the efforts, skills, encouragement and support of an amazing group of people. First the professionals: Liz Lisle, the publisher; Carey Jones, the editor; and Sarah Ciston, the designer. They took a rank amateur in hand and turned a lifetime of good recipes and ingredient lists into a real book. The friends: Bonnie Freeman, Kathleen Maegher, and Janice Cooper, who read, ate, and read some more. Thank you for pushing me to keep going. Thank you also to Margret Elson whose helpful advice moved me forward. Last but also first, my family: Josie for translating a lifetime of stories and cooking tips to the written page, and her husband Alex for tasting (and dish washing) from the Chicago campus. Endless appreciation to Molly for her legendary palate, for being the inspiration behind the vegetarian recipes, and for nagging me until I called Liz. Thanks to her husband (and cook) Jonathan for testing the recipes with a novice's eye and helping me clarify directions. Gratitude goes to Stephanie Gelb who created the whimsical illustrations throughout the book and provided critical editing advice (plus precious family recipes). All my love to Mark, who did the dishes and supported me all the way.

About the Authors

Marjorie Gelb has enjoyed finding and cooking wonderful recipes for more than forty years. Her professional colleagues know her as a full-time attorney who can make a mean chocolate dessert. Her children know her as a dedicated mother who can cook anything under the sun. Marjorie prepared dinner for her family every night of her working life (except when she had board meetings), and acquired her self-taught lazy cooking technique at the stovetop. As for the culinary basics, she picked those up while taking cooking classes at the Cordon Bleu in Paris, while studying with Countess Marie de Broglie in France, and from Josephine Araldo in San Francisco. Now she enjoys cooking on a smaller scale for herself and her husband, and sporadically on a larger scale for her family and friends.

Josie A. G. Shapiro learned that cooking is a relaxing, no-hassle joy at her mother's apron strings. Addicted to the wooden spoon at a young age, Josie graduated from the Cornell School of Hotel Administration, published a variety of articles on food and cooking, and is an avid Cooking Contester. Among other prizes, she won a month-long trip to France, several Slow Cookers, more aprons than she can count, and almost enough dollars in prize money to constitute a (very) part-time job. She works full time and prides herself on cooking lazy dinners for her husband, daughter, and various impromptu guests.

Stephanie Gelb is an architect and planner living and working in New York City. She is a recreational cook and as the parent of two children, taught herself to cut every cooking corner that she could. Her writing and drawing efforts have heretofore been limited to office memos and doing portraits of her unwilling colleagues at staff meetings.

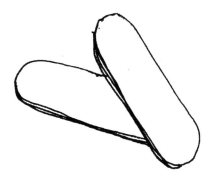

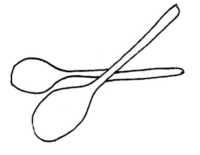